TAMING
THE
DIGITAL TIGER

TAMING
THE
DIGITAL TIGER

Judith Guertin
with
Barbara Hemphill

Taming the Digital Tiger

Printed in the United States of America

ISBN 978-1-946425-82-9

• WRITE WAY •
PUBLISHING COMPANY
RALEIGH, NORTH CAROLINA
www.writewaypublishingcompany.com

To my best friend, my partner,

and the dearest person I know,

my husband, Larry Guertin.

You cheered, supported, and loved me

through it all. Thank you. I love you!

Table of Contents

TAMING THE EMAIL TIGER
Gmail Edition

Preface

So many clients share that they are afraid to open their Inboxes. I know I am not the only one hearing these concerns. My fellow Certified Productive Environment Specialists™ tell me they hear it as well. We call it email overwhelm.

For over 40 years, Barbara Hemphill and the PEI consultants have helped clients "Tame the Paper Tiger." This brilliant work earned her the title "The Paper Tiger Lady." It is easy to find the Paper Tiger in your office: the paper piles, buried documents, boxes and bags of unidentified paper. Being stalked by this Tiger means you probably suffer from stress, sleepless nights, fear of losing your job, a client, and more.

I know many of you struggle with the Paper Tiger, but now, in addition to him, you face his cousin, the Digital Tiger. This ferocious feline is bigger and more insidious. He lurks behind every document you create, every email you send, receive, and every attachment. He steals your time, effort, energy, sleep, productivity, and peace of mind. He remains hidden, that is, until we try to find that one email that we need, right NOW.

Barbara and I created this guide for Taming the Tiger in your Gmail Inbox. We follow the same framework used in Tame the Paper Tiger: The Five Step Productive Environment Process.

BARBARA HEMPHILL'S WORDS OF WISDOM

You will find Barbara's 40+ years of wisdom in boxes like this throughout this guide. These include her sage advice and client reflections. She shares stories, proven techniques, and encouragement for your journey to Tame the Gmail Tiger.

Don't feel you need to read page by page. Pick and choose what you want to learn or brush up on. I will say it now and again throughout the book—this is a productivity buffet. Take what you want and leave the rest. Still hungry? Take another helping. No one else needs to know. Your secrets are safe with me.

To begin, you will need to know how to turn on the computer, go to the internet, go to Google, and open your Gmail account.

We divided this book into sections: 1) Where we are now 2) The Path to a Productive Environment™ Inbox in Five Steps 3) Your Methodology, 4) Mechanics: The Power of Systems, 5) Maintaining Your Inbox: Three Decisions for Success and 6) Maintenance.

We cover issues including: How did we get here? What problems do we face in our Inboxes? Why use Gmail? How can you transform your Inbox into a Productive Environment,™ an intentional setting where you can accomplish your work and enjoy your life?

We will show you what to do when life gets overwhelming and you lose control of your Inbox. We will give you steps you can take to return to order and sanity. You will find a wide variety of ways to customize your Gmail account to work most effectively for your situation and to help you maximize your productivity.

The Appendices will help you learn about using Search and the multitude of Keyboard Shortcuts you can use. There are so many ways to be more productive in Gmail.

Now, let's Tame that Gmail Tiger!

Judy

Introduction

Four decades ago, I began teaching individuals and organizations how to manage paper. Unfortunately, for many individuals and organizations, paper is still a problem, but people ignore it because "we've gone paperless." The same issues that plagued paper have now gone digital—with even more dangerous implications.

If you have a pile of 1,000 pieces of paper, and you need one, you can hire a temporary employee who knows nothing about your business to go through the pile looking for papers with certain words. If you have 1,000 digital documents, the challenge can be more significant. While the capability of search engines has wooed us, we now have to remember where the document is stored, on whose computer, what server, which platform. The result is a bigger, faster, hidden digital mess!

I base all my organizing efforts on four words: Clutter is Postponed Decisions®. What it took me three decades to figure out is why decision-making is so difficult for most of us. It all comes down to one word: fear. Fear that we will make a mistake, forget something, offend someone, miss an opportunity, or delete something, and want it back.

One principle that the company I founded, Productive Environment Institute, teaches is "Control what you can so you can cope with what you can't." Casual conversations and multiple surveys clarify that email is a significant cause of lost profit, productivity, and peace of mind. Companies spent millions of dollars introducing email, but they spent little money (and in most organizations, no money) training employees on how to use it to increase productivity.

Few companies create a protocol to manage their email, so employees have little or no control over how to manage email. Still, you *can* manage your email. Or at least you will be able to after you implement the strategies in this book. Caution: Perfectionism and procrastination will prevent progress! We base this book on many decades of real-world experience. It is not a "read once and put it on the shelf" book. Judy Guertin has designed it so you can improve your email skills every time you read it.

Clients often ask me, "What should I do?" to which Judy and I reply, "That is the wrong question. The real question is 'What WILL you do?'" Organizing doesn't have a right or wrong way—it is an art. We designed this book to help you identify and paint a picture of what you will do with your email.

Welcome to the journey!

Barbara

1. Where We Are Now

The colossal problem we face with email is the same problem we faced with paper . . .

CLUTTER
Is Postponed Decisions®

Our Inboxes are overflowing. Subject Lines like: Hi, RE your message, and FYI don't help. And what do we do with all those email attachments? Our Inboxes are growing every day, and we struggle just to stay afloat.

Are you running out of room in your Inbox?

What do we keep, where do we put it, and how will we find it when we need it again?

Barbara, aka "The Paper Tiger Lady," has been teaching us how to deal with the Paper Tiger for over 40 years. Her mantra is:

Today's Mail
Is Tomorrow's Pile™

You know that small stack of mail you left on the corner of your desk? Somehow it grew overnight into a bigger, messier, and more overwhelming pile. You didn't have the time to deal with it last week, yesterday, this morning, and most likely you won't have time later today either. It is a huge problem. If you are still struggling with the *Paper Tiger*, help is just a click away at the Productive Environment Network. In the network, we share the tools, systems, and strategies for dealing with him.

Today, however, you also face the Digital Tiger. He is lurking in your Inbox, your hard drive, cloud accounts, tablets, smartphones, and all those apps on your phone and tablets. Let's begin with email—to be more specific Gmail.

TODAY'S MAIL IS TOMORROW'S PILE™

One of the biggest mistakes clients make with any clutter is clearing it without creating a system to prevent it from happening again—or at the very least, making it far easier to recover.

When we dealt with the problems with paper files, we called them Paper Tigers: something appearing strong or fierce, but in reality being all show and no substance, weak, and nothing to be feared.

Now, our electronic files, especially our email Inboxes, have become "Digital Tigers." What we lack is the knowledge to tame them. We need systems, structure, and habits to master these digital carnivores to keep them from eating our time, space, energy, and money.

Do you feel stalked by the Digital Tiger? Did you know...

17% of us check email immediately upon getting up.[1]

_____

1) More Than Half of Americans Start Their Day by Checking Their Emails

The Tiger is sending us 180 NEW email items per day.[2] That equals at least 180 decisions to be made:

- Reply?
- Reply all?
- Delete?
- Keep?
- Who needs it?
- Where to save it?
- Add an attachment?
- Forward?
- Create a meeting?
- Create an appointment?

That is a lot of decisions!

Decision Fatigue

Quality of decisions

Number of decisions in a day

When you make so many, you risk "decision fatigue."[3] The more you make, the less time you take to make educated choices.

This is a huge problem, because as Barbara says, "Clutter is Postponed Decisions®."

By visiting your Inbox first thing, you use much of your good decision-making energy before you accomplish anything outside the Inbox.

How much energy will you have left to make important decisions later in the day? How many important items are postponed because you are worn out?

That tempting Tiger wants you to open that Inbox over and over. How many times per day do you open your Inbox? The average knowledge worker checks email more than 15 times per day,[4] costing 27 minutes per day simply opening and closing email.

2 Hiver Report on the state of Email in 2018
3 Decision Fatigue: What it is and how it's killing your motivation — RescueTime
4 Number of e-mails per day worldwide 2017-2023 Published by J. Clement

*In 2021, in the United States, you have 250 **working days**. If you lose 27 minutes per day on each working day, you will lose two hours and fifteen minutes per week. This totals five days over the course of one year, just opening and closing email. Think about it. What could you do with those five days? Vacation, training, signing up new clients or…?*

What about notifications? Your Digital Tiger sends you so many notifications! He loves making you lose focus! Keeping notifications turned on all day is the cause of significant loss of focus. Each time you respond to an alert (notification), it will take on average 23 minutes to return to your prior level of productivity.[5]

The state of your Inbox

Do you:

- Have thousands of emails in your Inbox because you have no idea where else to store them?
- Feel sick when you see the actual number of emails in your Inbox?
- Save email in locations within your email program other than your Inbox?
- Send them to tools outside Gmail like Trello, Evernote, OneNote, Keep, a CRM (Customer Relationship Manager), , or another Project Management tool?

---

5 You Lose Up To 25 Minutes Every Time You Respond To An Email

- Open and close the same emails over and over, only to realize you already read and possibly even responded to them?
- Lack a system for "processing" your email?
- Wonder what "processing email" means?!
- Fear that if the emails you receive are not kept in your Inbox, you will never find them again?

Are you ready for all that to change? Ready to Tame the Tiger in your Inbox?

LET'S GET ↙STARTED↘

The "byte" of the Digital Tiger

Do you keep all your emails in your Inbox? Does it make you feel safe knowing that they are "in there" somewhere? I am reminded of a client standing in front of a filing cabinet, looking for one document, saying the same thing, "It's in there somewhere." How will that help at all when there are 90,000 pieces of paper in that five-drawer filing cabinet? How will you find the one piece of paper you are looking for quickly, easily, and efficiently, if you ever find it at all?

If we apply the same principle to email, say for example Gmail, it has a 5GB Inbox. That Inbox could store as few as 500 10-megabyte emails or as many as 50,000 plain text emails.

No wonder we feel overwhelmed and need help! Watching my organizing clients work with their Inboxes, I can tell you that there is a lot of scrolling going on, looking for that one email. That is, until they learn how to tame their digital Inbox Tiger!

All change begins with the truth!

YOU CAN HAVE
ANYTHING
- BUT YOU CAN'T HAVE EVERYTHING

Gmail is not perfect—nor is any other email tool. If you have to use Gmail because it's required by your employer, then accept the fact and make it work. You can—this book will help you! If you can use another email tool, then, before you switch away from Gmail, make sure you are clear about what you do and don't like about it.

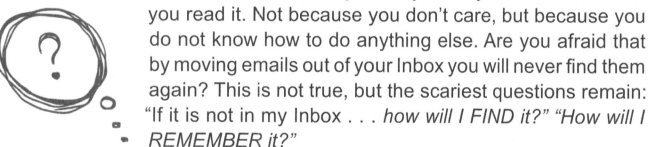

Is your Inbox your default archive? Every email just stays in the Inbox after you read it. Not because you don't care, but because you do not know how to do anything else. Are you afraid that by moving emails out of your Inbox you will never find them again? This is not true, but the scariest questions remain: "If it is not in my Inbox . . . *how will I FIND it?" "How will I REMEMBER it?"*

It is common for business owners to have a challenging relationship with email, whether it be the Webmail, iPhone Mail, Gmail, Outlook, Yahoo, or some other one. Some use multiple business accounts and don't forget the personal messages that flow through to their business email account.

Do you want your personal email mixed with your business email? Does email prevent you from accomplishing your most important tasks at work?

You need to decide whether you want this to continue and determine how you want to view these accounts.

So, you decided (or your Company decided for you) to use Gmail for your email provider. Remember, no matter which tool you choose, not everyone will agree with your choice. Your colleagues and friends may use something else. They tell you their favorite has bigger, better bells and whistles. Maybe their choice has more features, maybe it doesn't. Maybe you need these features, maybe you don't. Just because other tools have a new feature, that does not mean you need it. If you think you need a feature you just learned about, don't just assume your tool does not have the same option. It may be worth a bit of research to find out.

Tools are updated all the time. Gmail is no exception—new features and functions are added regularly.

Are you always on the lookout for the "perfect tool?" Isn't that a waste of time and money? There is no such thing as a perfect tool. There are many that are "good enough." A tool that will work for most of your tasks. When you find one that is good enough, adopt it, use it, and get comfortable with it. Stop risking the loss of important data you left in a program you stopped using. Whether you use Gmail or something else, there will be NO "perfect" email provider. However, there will be one that will get the job done. One you can work with at a deep level. Invest the time now to learn how to use Gmail to its fullest.

Remember, the scariest question related to email is *"How will I find it when I need it?"*

2. The Path to a Productive Environment Inbox in Five Steps

1 STATE YOUR VISION

In this first step, you will define what your ideal email system will look like, how it will function, and how you will access it.

Here are some questions to get you started developing your Vision.

What part does email play in your overall **internal** (within your company) communication process? Is this the main avenue for communication within your company, or do you use something else for day-to-day communications like Slack, Telegram, or some other Chat tool?

What part does email play in your **external** communications with clients, colleagues, vendors, and referral partners? Is this how work orders are submitted or does this happen in another tool? How about service requests? Are Help Tickets submitted or are help requests made via email?

What communications are best served in email? As Guy Kawasaki, former Chief Evangelist at Apple and current Chief Evangelist at Canva, the graphic design giant, says, *"The purpose of email is to save time, not kill time."*

How much of your email is read and acted upon? When you reply to an email, are your replies brief and to the point? Do they lead the recipient to take a specific action?

 It is important to be brief, specific, and most of all, realistic. Current studies show that on average, we spend only 13.4 seconds reading an email. Just 13.4 seconds!

Does your organization suffer from "but we have always done it that way syndrome"? Do members of your team resist change? Does your organization have an epidemic of 's (carbon copies) and 's (blind carbon copies)? Often, people do this to cover their butt(s). This practice clogs Inboxes, wastes time, and consumes server space at an alarming rate.

The same is true for the use, or overuse, of Reply All. Many people use it to show how hard they are working on a project or how well they dealt with an issue.

In fact, studies show it costs an organization 95 cents every time we open an email.[6] So, it costs almost $1 every time someone in your organization reads an email that they should not have received—an email that was sent to "cover the bases" or because the sender could not be bothered to figure out who really needed that content. Is this cost effective for your company?

- Do you have established naming conventions to quickly and clearly distinguish projects and actions needed?
- Do you use notifications?
- How many times a day do you look at email?
- Do you have a policy for dealing with Attachments?
- Under what circumstances would you forward an email?

Take a few minutes to think about and write your vision for your email client.

- How do you see it working in your business?
- How will your Inbox look?
- When will it be open?
- Will you have established email processes and procedures?
- Where will you store email that you need to save?
- What does your Inbox look like at the end of the day?
- What would have to happen in order for you to solve your email problem?
- How will you feel if you solve this problem?

Don't worry if you do not have all the answers to these questions just yet. Let's keep going before the Tiger gets any closer!

---

6 Email Is Not Free

2 IDENTIFY AND ELIMINATE YOUR OBSTACLES

An obstacle is anything that impedes doing the work you need to do. Here are some we encounter all the time. Which ones are getting in *your* way? Maybe you have even come across some that are not on this list!

Here is where the Digital Tiger is hiding in the bushes, waiting to pounce on your productivity:

- Not understanding the capabilities of your email program beyond Send, Receive, Forward, and Delete
- Using the Inbox as your archive
- Adopting new or additional tools that duplicate features of tools you already own
- The never-ending quest for the *perfect tool*
- Being given a new email program to use with no training or methodology for using it
- Lacking specific, consistently utilized naming conventions
- Creating too much information; too many copies. (I read somewhere that for every original email there are 19 copies being kept. Some of us even PRINT emails so we don't lose them)
- Not knowing which emails are required for regulatory, legal, and tax purposes, leading to keeping them all
- Not using Conversation View (How else do you know the email you are responding to is the most current message)

- Scrolling instead of using the Search function . . . up and down, up and down
- Using email for all internal communications
- Too many people saving copies of emails that contain attachments
- CYB, covering your butt by Cc'ing, or even worse Bcc'ing, everyone in your organization to immunize yourself against blame or to prove dedication to a project or a team
- Insufficient backup strategy for hardware and software
- Interruptions because of Notifications
- Read/Re-read (Open/Close, Open/Close . . .)
- Not deleting Spam Mail or marking items as such. Not training Gmail which messages to filter by moving them to the Spam Label
- Overusing Reply All
- Getting Read Receipts, more cover-your-butts
- Indecision—not sure what to do with an email (postponed decisions)
- *Spending 13.4 seconds, the average read time, on an unnecessary email*
- Covering too many topics in one email–leading to many of them never being responded to and to creating still more emails to obtain the answers to remaining questions/concerns
- Using too many labels, or not having the right labels. (Don't worry if you are not familiar with Labels just yet. If you are familiar with Folders in other programs, labels are similar. More on labels is coming soon.)

Now take a few minutes to identify and list your obstacles. Once you understand what is getting in your way, you can get started eliminating them. Yes, write them down. Putting them on paper will help you to focus.

3 COMMIT YOUR RESOURCES

THE COST FACTOR

Are you concerned about hiring an expert to help out of fear they will make you throw everything away? Here's my philosophy: You can keep everything you want if you are willing to pay the price in time, space, money, and energy. My job is to help you understand the cost so you can make an educated decision that will help you accomplish your work and enjoy your life.™

Let's talk about your resources:

Time

- Schedule time on your calendar to create your system.
- Review your Inbox and decide what to delete.
- Plan regular time on your calendar to **process** your Inbox. Find more on processing elsewhere in this guide.
- If you have a large backlog of emails that needs processing, plan blocks of time to accomplish this task rather than trying to do it all at once.

 Space

- If you run out of storage, you will either need to delete some saved emails or buy more storage. It is possible some of you will need to do both.
- By clearing your email Inbox of junk/spam and no longer needed items, you will reclaim space or eliminate the need to add additional storage.
- Be sure you empty the Trash. In Gmail, items you send to the trash today will remain there for 30 days unless you manually empty the Trash. The space they occupy in your account will not change until you empty the Trash or contents are removed by the 30-day rule.

⚡ Energy

- Creating systems and setting times to deal with the backlog will take a lot of energy.
- When will you feel fresh and ready to make decisions about each email?

💰 Money

- How much does it cost when you don't fully understand how to use your email program? Lost opportunities, missed responses, broken trust, customers going to your competition? In the long run, the money spent on hiring a trainer to help you get the most from your email client is well worth the investment.
- Is it just you clearing your Inbox, or will all the members of your team be clearing theirs too? Invest in some training for them as well.

WHAT A DIFFERENCE A FEW HOURS CAN MAKE!

One of my clients, a company of 400 employees, was getting ready to move and was in the process of going paperless. I led an event where each employee focused for one day on clearing the clutter prior to the move. We spent half the day clearing physical clutter and half the day focusing on their digital clutter. At the end of the day, nearly one-half of their digital files were deleted. One of the executives was able to reduce her inbox from 24,000 to 4,000 emails.

Now it is your turn. How many of these resources (or others) will *you* need to apply to solve *your* Inbox overwhelm? Everyone is different, so your mileage may vary.

4 DESIGN AND IMPLEMENT YOUR PLAN

Okay, so far you have stated your vision, identified and eliminated your obstacles, and committed your resources. Now it's time to create your plan.

PRODUCTIVE ENVIRONMENT™
7 Information Management Questions

Let's begin by answering these important questions.

1. Which emails do you need to keep? (Examples: Historical, Tax, Legal)
2. In what form—Archive, Labels, Categories, Stars or in another tool such as OneNote, Evernote, Asana, Trello?
3. For how long? Create a Retention Policy for your business and follow as written.
4. Who is responsible for filing or archiving? Do you need to keep FYI emails? Do you need to keep every email you were Cc'd or Bcc'd on?
5. Who needs access to the email you have saved? Are they in shared Folders, on the company server, or in Cloud storage?
6. How can they be found? Have Labels, Categories, or Stars been used?
7. How is it backed up? Local hard drive, Cloud Accounts, and/or External Drive?

Don't have the answers yet? More information to help you answer these questions is in the coming pages.

5 SUSTAIN YOUR SUCCESS

Now that you have completed the process of creating your vision, eliminating your obstacles, committing your resources, and designing and implementing your plan, you are ready for the most important step of all: sustaining your success!

In this step, you will review your Inbox according to your plan. Here is where life gets interesting. What if something comes up that makes it difficult to follow through? Do you give up? Tell yourself you will deal with it later? Do you feel helpless? Well, my friends, none of these actions are necessary. You have the perfect tool to help you find the answer: The Five Step-Productive Environment Process™. Whenever you hit a roadblock or a new obstacle, go back to the five steps to guide you.

Step 1. State your vision.
- Is your vision still the same? If so, go to step 2. If not, clarify, and state your (new) Vision.

Step 2. Identify and eliminate your obstacles.
- Did you discover new obstacles? What are they? How will you eliminate them?

Step 3. Commit your resources.
- Do you need to add any new resources to your plan? Do you need more time, space, energy, or money?

Step 4. Design and implement your new plan.
- What changes do you need to make? What is different this time?

Step 5. Sustain your success.
- Schedule a regular time to check that all is well with the new plan.

Any time you feel stuck, revisit the process to reset and restart. You may not need to go all the way back to Step 1, but you can if you need to. It is a circular plan, so you can move between the elements any time you find a stumbling block.

3. Your Methodology

Methodology is the system you use to process your email. To be clear, processing is not the same as skimming, checking, or peeking at your Inbox. When you **process** your email, you look at each one, take the next action and move it out of your Inbox. (We will discuss more about where the email goes when you move it out of the Inbox in a moment.)

Repeat after me: my Gmail Inbox is not my calendar, my task (To-Do) list, or my filing system.

Processing your inbox

Your Inbox is where UNPROCESSED email goes. When you go to your Inbox, you will **process** email.

To prepare for processing email, first you must answer some important questions. Do you:

- Have a plan for when will you process your Inbox? Do you process in the morning, afternoon, at midday, end of day, or some combination? How many times per day is sufficient?
- Have certain times of the day when you feel you can focus and make the necessary decisions about the email in your Inbox?
- Understand the expectations of your organization regarding how quickly to reply to someone who makes a request via email: 24 hours, 48 hours, or some other time frame?
- Know how to create and use email signatures?
- Include a message in your email signature about when you deal with email and how to reach you in an emergency?
- Have a system to read your email? Do you "read only" on your phone and "reply" from your laptop? Do you read on your smartwatch and/or receive notifications there?
- Have your Inbox open at all times?
- Have Notifications turned on?
- Understand when to Reply to one person in a conversation vs. when to use Reply All to everyone in the conversation?

- Know when to Forward an email conversation vs. including someone new in a conversation?
- Have a system to handle attachments? Do you remove the files and store them separately? Do you remove them when you reply to a message? Can you remove them?
- Archive all messages that contain an attachment?
- Know where to save attachments so you can find them when you need them?

Make note of what you do now. As we move on, you will decide how to implement your new system. This is your starting point.

What are the benefits of using Gmail?

 Gmail is a web-based tool, available across platforms. So, when you process email on one platform (like your laptop, your tablet, or cell phone, for example), it syncs on the other platforms. No deleting on multiple devices or wondering if you have responded to an email or not.

There are multiple ways to categorize the items in your Inbox. These include labels, stars, and filters which are available on all platforms (Mac, PC, IOS, Android).

Gmail plays well with all of the Google Workspace tools. If you use other Google Workspace tools like Google Drive, Google Docs, Google Sheets, Google Keep, Google Tasks, and Google Slides, you have a compelling reason to use Gmail.

There are also non-Google tools available that you can add to the Inbox Side Panel (more on the Side Panel in a bit). These allow you to act right from within your Inbox! Tools like Box, Dropbox, Zoom, and many others can be added to the Side Panel. (Some tools may not be available if you are on a Mac, but in the PC environment you will have many choices available.)

Whether you are a current user or a novice, we hope that you will use this book to create a vision for your Gmail account and how it fits into your digital toolbox.

4. Mechanics: The Power of Systems

THE POWER OF SYSTEM
Saving You Space Time Energy Money

I learned early in my career that Clutter is Postponed Decisions®
but it was several years before a colleague said that it's not
enough to make the decision. You have to have a way to
implement it.

Let's customize your email Inbox settings to work best for you.

Here are some simple ways to customize your email Inbox to work best FOR YOU. You'll even learn how to connect email to other tools you use without ever leaving the Inbox screen.

Typically, users know only a handful of functions in their email program (otherwise known as their email client). They can Send, Receive, Forward, and Delete. Gmail offers many customizations to make your working procedures more streamlined and to make processing your email easier and more intuitive. Experts will tell you to work smarter, not harder! Would you like to schedule appointments, check your calendar, make notes for later, or add items to a task list right from your Inbox?

As this guide introduces the various customizations available, remember that we do not all work the same way, and some of the customizations may not appeal to you or may not function well with how you like to work. Customizations are designed to give you the look and feel that you want to see in your Inbox. Many of them will decrease repetitive tasks, help you locate important items in seconds, and integrate with other programs that you need and use every day.

Think of customizations as a productivity buffet. Select what you like and leave the rest. This is OK. Your system needs to work for you, not for us, or for anyone else, just you!

Our goal is to share with you the tools you need to harness the full power of Gmail. Given that more and more business owners and entrepreneurs are turning to Gmail, this is a great time to learn more about the enormous capabilities you have from right within the Gmail interface.

Customization Basics: Getting started with Gmail — Select your settings for Inbox success

You may already understand many of the functionalities that Gmail has to offer, but even if you do, take this time to review and remind yourself of some time-saving ways you can use Gmail.

If you are comfortable with how Settings work in your Gmail Account, you may prefer to go right to the Managing Your Inbox–Three Decisions for Success section in this book.

Your avatar

Locate your Avatar on the upper right of the screen. If you upload a photo to Google, you will see it here. If you do not have a photo saved, you will see an icon in place of a photo.

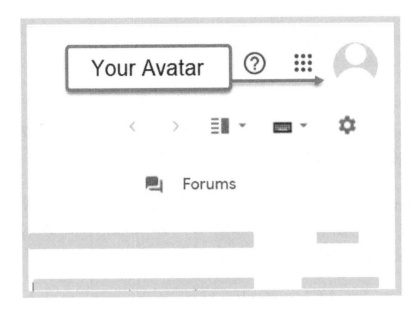

If you have more than one Gmail account, clicking on your Avatar will reveal a drop-down list of your other linked accounts. Click on the one you need when you want to switch between accounts.

In the example below, number one is the account being viewed. To change to the default account, click on the area where the number two is shown. The word *Default* will appear next to the name in the default account. Number 2 in this example.

From this same screen you can also go to your Google account settings. Click on Manage your Google Account.

Click on your Avatar to view your Google-wide settings. These settings apply to: Google Docs, Google Sheets, Google Keep, and all the other Google Apps. Just remember, when making changes in Settings, ALWAYS scroll to the bottom of the page and click SAVE CHANGES.

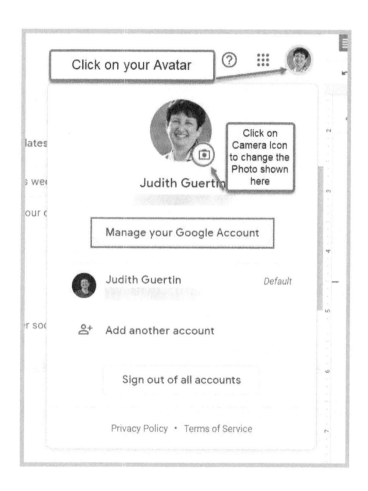

Click on the Camera Icon to change your profile picture.

The choices are **Upload photos**, select from **Your Photos**, or **Drag a photo** to the box on the screen below. Then, click in the lower left, **Set as profile photo**.

If you have another Gmail Account and you want to connect them together, click on Add another account. To get started, sign in to Google. On the top right, select your profile image or initial. From the menu, choose Add account, then follow the instructions to sign in to the account you want to use.

To switch between accounts, on the top right, select your profile image or your Avatar. Then from the list, select the account you'd like to use.

Customizing Gmail to look and feel natural for how you like to work is our first task. To make changes, go to the Gear Icon on the upper right, and click on it.

Settings (gear Icon)

To make changes to the look and feel of Gmail, after you click the **Gear Icon**, open the **Quick Settings** area. Click on **See all settings**. There are several tabs in Settings. The other choices available from the **Gear Icon** include changing the **Display Density**, changing the **Themes, Inbox Type, Reading Pane, and Email Threading.**

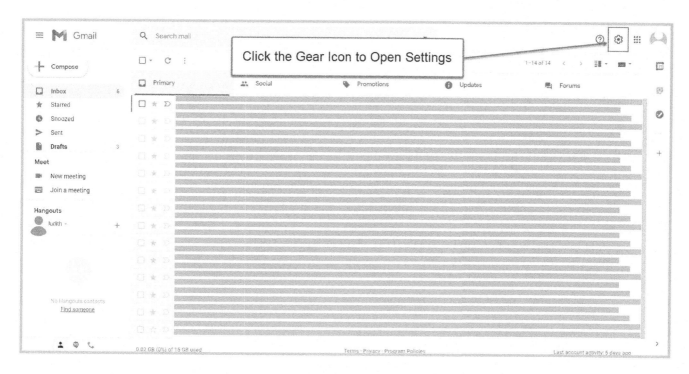

Options from the Gear Icon

Click the **Gear Icon**, then click on **See all settings**. You will see the following tabs:

- General
- Labels
- Inbox
- Accounts and Import

- Filters and Blocked Addresses

- Forwarding POP/IMAP
- Add-ons
- Chat and Meet

- Advanced
- Offline
- Themes

To begin, let's explore some of the Settings in the **General Tab**. Use this as an overview of some of the features available. We will discuss many of my favorites more in depth throughout the book.

General Tab

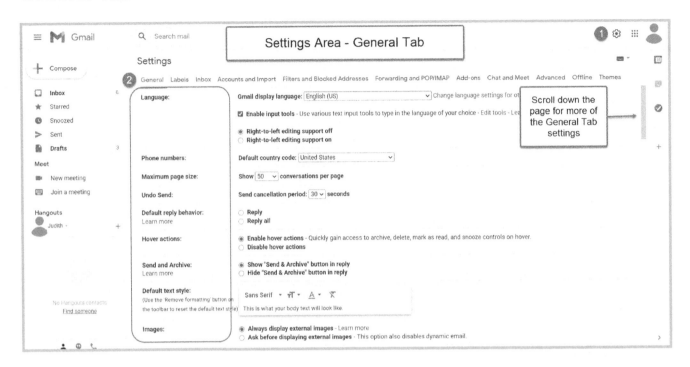

Language: Make your selection from the drop-down list.

Language:	Gmail display language: English (US) ⌄ Change language settings for other Google products
	☑ **Enable input tools** - Use various text input tools to type in the language of your choice - Edit tools - Learn more
	⦿ **Right-to-left editing support off** ○ **Right-to-left editing support on**

Phone numbers: Select your country code for Phone numbers.

Phone numbers:	Default country code: United States ⌄

Maximum Page Size: Choose from 10, 15, 20, 25, 50, or 100 per page.

Phone numbers:	**Number of emails per page**	⌄
Maximum page size:	Show 50 ⌄ conversations per page	
	10	
	15	
Undo Send:	Send c 20 ion period: 30 ⌄ seconds	
	25	
Default reply behavior:	○ Re 50	
Learn more	○ Re 100	

Undo Send: Set the length of time from five to 30 seconds for recalling a sent message.

Undo Send:	Send cancellation period: 5 ▾ seconds

Default reply behavior: Reply or Reply All. Select Reply as your default versus Reply All. Reply All should be reserved for those instances when replying to all is truly necessary. You can select Reply All on an email by email basis when you have a compelling reason to do so.

Default reply behavior:	○ Reply
Learn more	○ Reply all

Hover actions: Hovering your mouse over an email in the list, without opening it, will show the Archive, Delete, Mark as Read, and Snooze buttons.

Hover actions:	◉ **Enable hover actions** - Quickly gain access to archive, delete, mark as read, and snooze controls on hover.
	○ **Disable hover actions**

Send and Archive: You can add a Send and Archive button to your email so that you can complete these actions in one step. This email can then be found in the All Mail Label, where all Archived mail is stored.

Default text style: Select your Font, Size, Text Color or Remove Formatting.

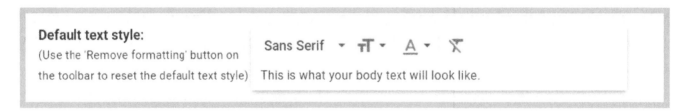

Images: What to do with External Images. Decide if you want external images to be shown or if you want to be asked before displaying the images. Do you trust that all images are benign, or do you want to make a choice each time?

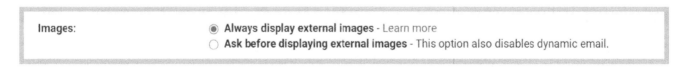

Dynamic email: Used to quickly compose Replies to events, fill out Questionnaires, Browse Catalogs, Respond to Comments, Update emails to display the latest content.

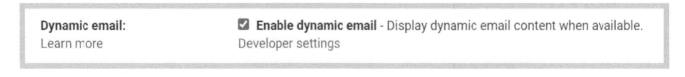

Grammar: Turn grammar suggestions on or off.

> Grammar:
>
> ◉ **Grammar suggestions on**
> ◯ **Grammar suggestions off**

Spelling: Turn spelling suggestions on or off.

> Spelling:
>
> ◉ **Spelling suggestions on**
> ◯ **Spelling suggestions off**

Auto-advance: After you archive, delete, or mute a conversation, you have three choices: move to the next conversation in the list, move to the previous conversation in the list, or go back to the thread list.

> Auto-advance:
>
> **After archiving, deleting, muting, etc. a conversation:**
> ◉ **Go to the next (newer) conversation**
> ◯ **Go to the previous (older) conversation**
> ◯ **Go back to the threadlist**

Autocorrect: Gmail will make corrections for you. Choose On or Off.

> Autocorrect:
>
> ◉ **Autocorrect on**
> ◯ **Autocorrect off**

Smart Compose: Gmail will offer suggestions based on your writing style while you compose an email.

> **Smart Compose:**
> (predictive writing suggestions appear as you compose an email)
>
> ◉ **Writing suggestions on**
> ◯ **Writing suggestions off**
> Feedback on Smart Compose suggestions

Smart Compose personalization: Gmail will offer personalized suggestions based on your writing style.

> **Smart Compose personalization:** ◉ **Personalization on**
> (Smart Compose is personalized to your ○ **Personalization off**
> writing style)

Experimental Access: Gain early access to features Google is trying out in Gmail. *Note: since these are experimental, they can disappear without notice.

> **Experimental Access:** ☐ **Enable experimental access** - Gain early access to features still under development. Google may email you
> Learn more to request feedback on these features. Experimental features (indicated by ⚗) may be removed without notice.

Conversation View: Conversation threads group an email and all activity associated with it in one view. The newest reply is shown at the bottom of the thread. This way you see the most recent activity related to this topic without having to scroll, hoping you have selected the most current message.

Note there is a limit of 100 conversations per thread.

> **Conversation View:** ◉ **Conversation view on**
> (sets whether emails of the same topic ○ **Conversation view off**
> are grouped together)

Nudges: Gmail will suggest replying to email you may have forgotten about or need to follow up on.

> **Nudges:** ☑ **Suggest emails to reply to** - Emails you might have forgotten to respond to will appear at the top of your inbox
> Learn more ☑ **Suggest emails to follow up on** - Sent emails you might need to follow up on will appear at the top of your inbox

Smart Reply: Suggested replies to your email. You can choose to turn on or off. To accept a reply that Gmail suggests, use the tab key on your keyboard to accept. The cursor will move to the end of the suggested reply, and you can continue typing from there.

Smart Reply:	◉ **Smart Reply on**
(Show suggested replies when available.)	○ **Smart Reply off**

Preview Pane: When you view an email in the Preview Pane, decide how many seconds of previewing will mark it as read. You can choose from immediately to never. The default setting is 20 seconds.

Preview Pane:

Mark a conversation as read: After 3 seconds ▾
- Immediately
- After 1 second
- After 3 seconds
- After 20 seconds
- Never

Desktop notifications: Click here to enable desktop notifications for Gmail.
(allows Gmail to display popup   ○ **New mail notifications on** - Notify me when any new message arrives in my inbox or primary tab
notifications on your desktop when new   ○ **Important mail notifications on** - Notify me only when an important message arrives in my inbox
email messages arrive)   ◉ **Mail notifications off**
Learn more

Desktop notifications: Do you want notifications? You can choose from: New mail, Important mail, or Mail notifications off. Instead of relying on notifications, schedule times to open and process your email. *Notifications can be shown on some devices but not others by going to the settings on each device to turn on or off.

Desktop notifications: Click here to enable desktop notifications for Gmail.
(allows Gmail to display popup   ○ **New mail notifications on** - Notify me when any new message arrives in my inbox or primary tab
notifications on your desktop when new   ○ **Important mail notifications on** - Notify me only when an important message arrives in my inbox
email messages arrive)   ◉ **Mail notifications off**
Learn more

Stars: If color is useful in your system, there are a full 12 Stars to allow users to search by colored icons. Select none, one, all, or any number in between, whatever works for you.

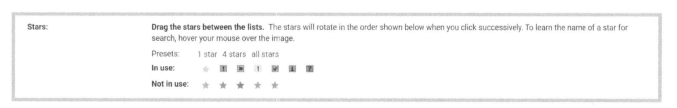

Stars:
Drag the stars between the lists. The stars will rotate in the order shown below when you click successively. To learn the name of a star for search, hover your mouse over the image.

Presets: 1 star   4 stars   all stars

In use: ⭐ 🟦 🟦 ❗ ☑ 🟦 ❓

Not in use: ★ ★ ★ ★ ★

Keyboard shortcuts: Stop wasting time repeatedly reaching for the mouse. It is faster to enable these shortcuts and keep your hands on the keyboard. Start with a few you like and build your repertoire over time. You will find shortcuts for computers, Android, and iPhone/iPad. Look for a list of keyboard shortcuts in Appendix 1 at the end of this book.

Keyboard shortcuts:
Learn more

○ **Keyboard shortcuts off**
◉ **Keyboard shortcuts on**

Button labels: If you have a hard time remembering what the icons mean, you have the choice of changing them to text. For instance, instead of a trash can icon you will see the word Delete.

Button labels:
Learn more

◉ **Icons**
○ **Text**

My picture: How to add a picture to your profile. This will be shown for your Avatar across all Google Apps.

My picture:
Learn more

Your Google profile picture is visible across Google services. You can change your picture in About me.

Create contacts for auto-complete: You have two choices. When you send a message to a new person, Gmail will automatically add them to "Other Contacts" to enable Gmail to auto-complete the To: field with their email address the next time you want to send them an email. The other choice is for you to open a new contact record and add the email address and other contact information manually.

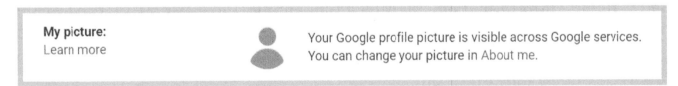

Create contacts for auto-complete: ◉ When I send a message to a new person, add them to Other Contacts so that I can auto-complete to them next time
○ I'll add contacts myself

Importance signals for ads: Click on the word "here" to see how advertisements are personalized for you. You can edit or turn off this feature. In any event, you will still receive ads, but turning this off will eliminate the personalized ads.

Signature: Create your email signature here. Add your name, address, phone number, email, links to your website, and more. With this turned on, your contact information is added to the new email messages you compose.

Personal level indicators: You can choose not to show indicators or to show indicators. When you show indicators, a single Arrow (>) is for messages sent to your address and a group of others. Double arrows (>>) show messages sent only to you. No arrows are displayed if the email is sent from a mailing list.

Snippets: Choose to see the subject only or a bit of the text of the email.

Vacation responder: Create an automatic reply that Gmail uses to respond to incoming messages when you are on vacation. Choose the check box at the bottom to limit this message to only people in your Contacts. By limiting this reply to your contacts, you lessen the possibility of publicizing news of your vacation with those outside your known contacts. You can let your contacts know when you will be away and provide them a contact during your absence. When you return from vacation, return to **Settings**, **General tab** and select **Vacation responder off**.

To apply the changes, click the Save Changes at the bottom of the page in Settings.

Other options from the Gear Icon

Display Density

From the Gear Icon ⚙ see three **Display Density** options: Default, Comfortable, and Compact layout options. Changing the **Display Density** will show you more or less space between items in the Inbox and on the screen. Click each choice to preview. When you find the one you like, click OK. If you are not happy with your choice, you can always return to the **Gear Icon** and change it again.

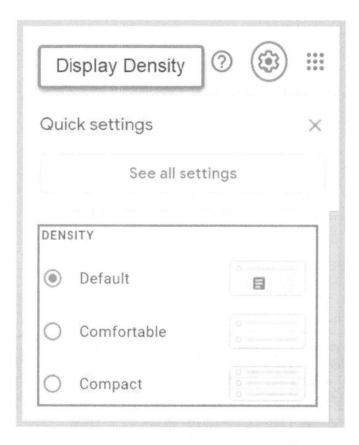

Themes

Tired of the basic Gmail background? Need some inspiration? Try changing your theme. Click the **Gear Icon** to reveal Quick Settings. Scroll down and see if you like one of the eight choices. Want more choices? Click on View all. Still not inspired? Choose one of your own photos stored in your Google Photos. Click on My Photos to use a photo of your own that you saved to Google Photos.

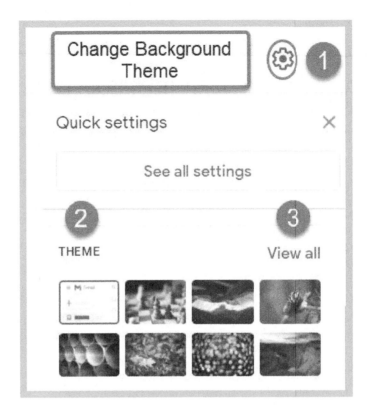

To go directly to settings for all the choices, click See all settings.

Change your Theme as often as you like.

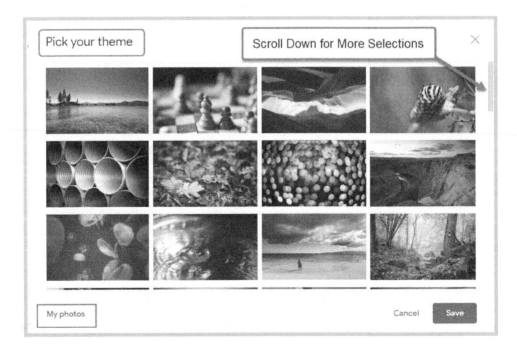

New Background Theme chosen (top left, in the previous screenshot).

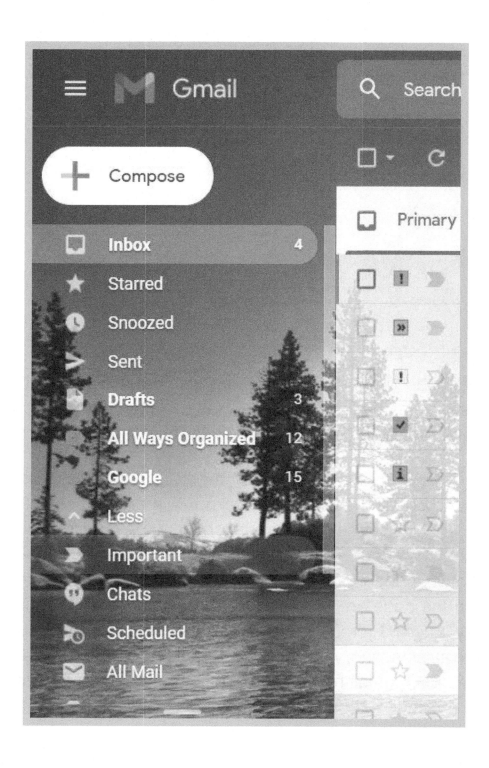

Tour of the Inbox

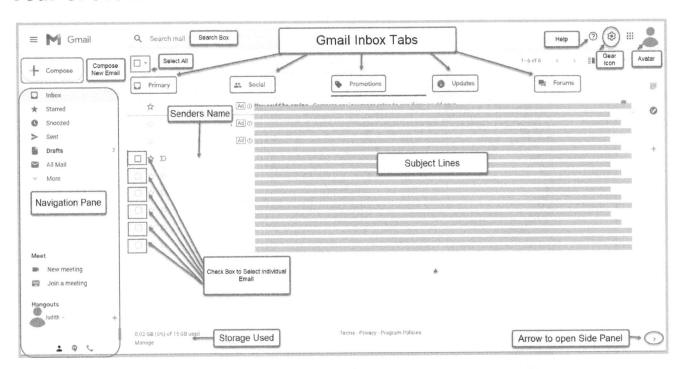

At the top left side of Inbox is the Compose Button for writing new email. Below this is the Navigation Pane: view labels, empty spam, start a Chat or Google Meet, manage labels, create new labels, and empty Trash.

In the center of the screen is the Search box at the top. Just below that is the check box for Select all. When checked, this box will select all email on this page. Your choice in settings dictates how many emails appear per page (10, 15, 20, 25, 50 or 100). The total number of pages is shown to the right; the < > move between the Inbox pages. Show the oldest first or the newest first. Moving down the page are the inbox divisions. On this screen is the default view: Primary, Social, Promotions, Updates, and Forums. Below that is the list of email in the selected tab, with sender's name, preview (if selected in settings) and time sent. Each email has a check box in front of it on the list. Use check box to select an email. At bottom is the amount of storage used in your account.

The right side of the screen begins at the top with the Help button, the Waffle button to select other Google apps, your Avatar, the **Gear Icon**, the Preview button, and the Input tool. At the very bottom is the side panel pop out arrow. When selected, you will see icons for Google Calendar, Google Keep, Google Tasks and other tools you can add from Google Workspace Marketplace.

Inbox view options

The Default Inbox is the one you see when you open a new Gmail account. To make changes to the Inbox view, go to the **Gear Icon**, then click Settings, then click on the Inbox tab.

Default View divides up the incoming email we receive into five categories:

- ☑ Primary
- ☑ Social
- ☑ Promotion
- ☑ Updates
- ☑ Forums

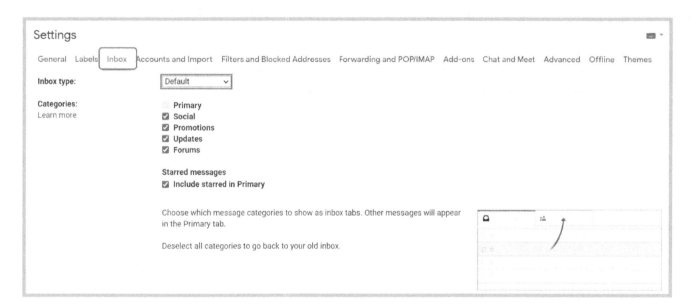

Select the categories you wish to use for your Inbox. In this example, we selected them all by clicking on the check box in front of the Category Name. Only those you select will be shown at the top of your Inbox as seen here.

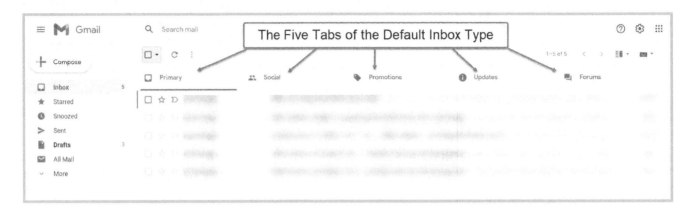

You are free to use all of these or as few as you need to understand the mail you receive in your Inbox. If Forums are not something you receive, uncheck the box to turn off this tab. It will place any mail that would have been sent to the Forums tab in your Primary Inbox.

You have other options for the **Inbox types**. To change to a different Inbox view, go to the drop-down list and click on the down arrow ▼. We will cover many of these choices as we continue.

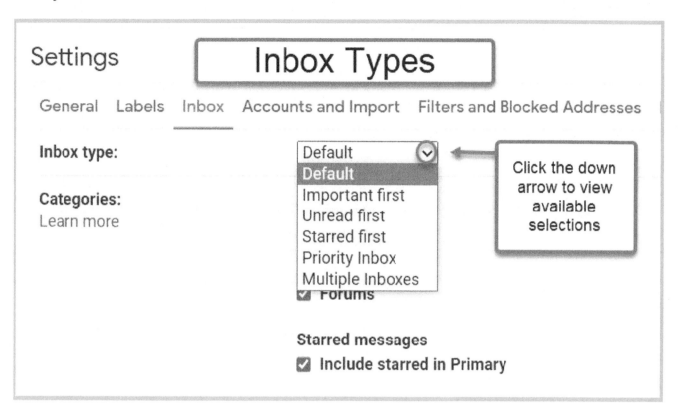

Select from the drop-down list the choice you would like to try. You can return to this setting over and over and try all the choices until you find the one you like the best.

Train your tabs

No matter which Inbox View you use, Gmail decides which tab an email belongs in based on an algorithm. It decides based on how you interacted with similar emails in the past. If you find an email is mis-categorized, drag it to the correct tab (the one you want it delivered to). You will see a notification at the lower left of the screen asking if you want this to apply to new email coming from this address. In most cases if you are moving an email to a different tab, the answer will be yes.

It is especially important to move emails that do not belong in the Primary tab, out of the Primary tab to the proper tab. This way, Gmail will deliver only the most important email to your Primary tab.

Let's continue with the other views you can select from for your Inbox. Try each Inbox and choose the best fit for you. The next view option is:

Important First view

Select Important first from ▼

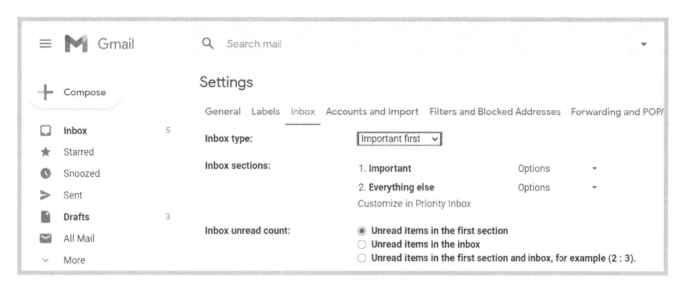

Don't forget to click **Save Changes** at the bottom of the page to apply the changes.

Your Inbox will now have two sections: **Important** and **Everything else.** This is how the Inbox will appear.

If there are new emails, you will see them in the appropriate category. In the same manner, the Inbox learns what is important. Using the "**Important Marker**" will make this view more valuable over time. Gmail makes the important determination based on an algorithm of how you interact with your email. By choosing the "**Important Marker**" on an email, you are telling Gmail this email belongs in the **Important Inbox** and the **Important Label**.

If you wish to use this feature, be sure it is turned on in **Settings, Inbox label, Importance markers**.

Importance markers: ● **Show markers** - Show a marker ( ) by messages marked as important.
⊙ **No markers**

Gmail analyzes your new incoming messages to predict what's
important, considering things like how you've treated similar messages
in the past, how directly the message is addressed to you, and many
other factors. Learn more

● Use my past actions to predict which messages are important to me.
⊙ Don't use my past actions to predict which messages are important.
  Note: this will erase action history and will likely reduce the accuracy of importance predictions.

The Importance marker is the Yellow arrow next to the emails in the Important Label. Here is what it looks like in your Inbox:

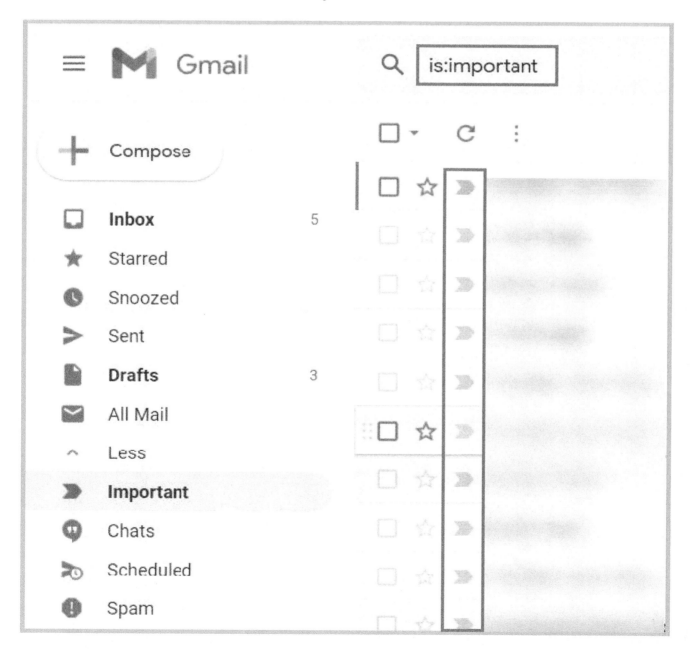

Unread First view

To select this view, go to **Gear Icon**, **See all settings**, **Inbox tab**, **Inbox type**, and click the drop-down and select **Unread first**. The categories in this Inbox: **Unread** and **Everything else**.

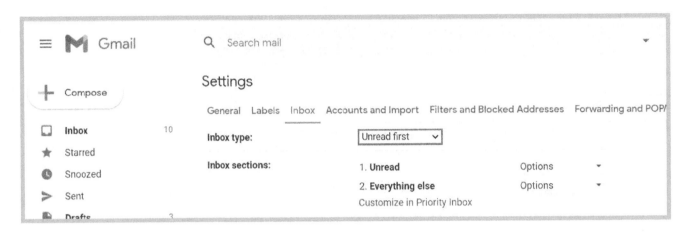

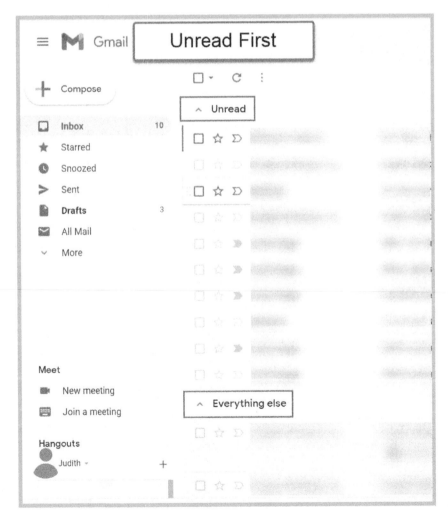

Starred First view

To select this view, go to **Gear Icon**, **See all settings**, **Inbox tab**, **Inbox type**, and click the drop-down and select **Starred first**. The categories in this Inbox: **Starred** and **Everything else**.

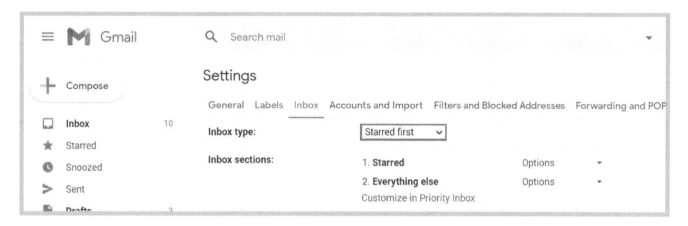

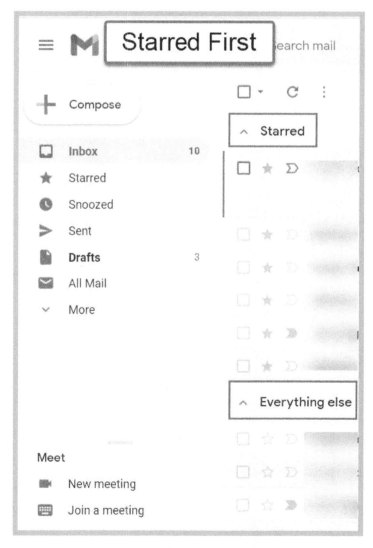

Priority Inbox view

To select this view, go to **Gear Icon**, **See all settings**, **Inbox tab**, **Inbox type**, and click the drop-down and select **Priority Inbox**. The categories in this Inbox: **Important and unread, Starred, Empty** and **Everything else**.

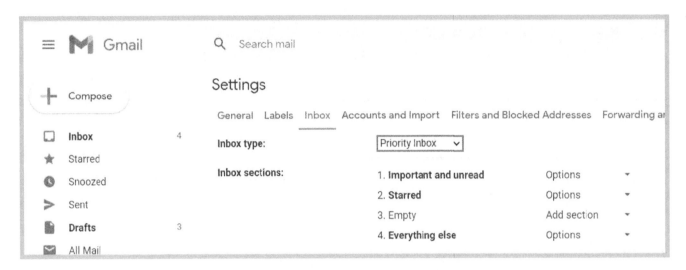

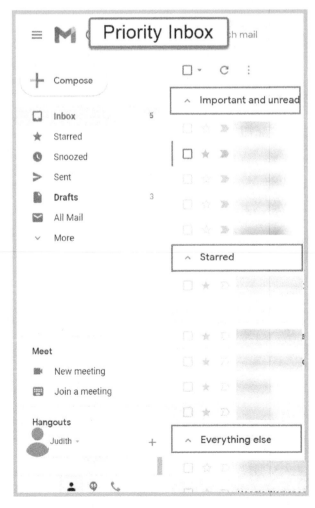

The section named **Empty** is one that you can customize with categories important to you. Click the drop-down to see your options. Add this section only if it is useful to your system.

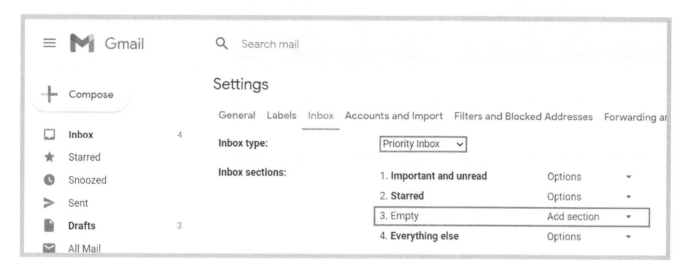

The example shown above is without adding the "Empty" Section.

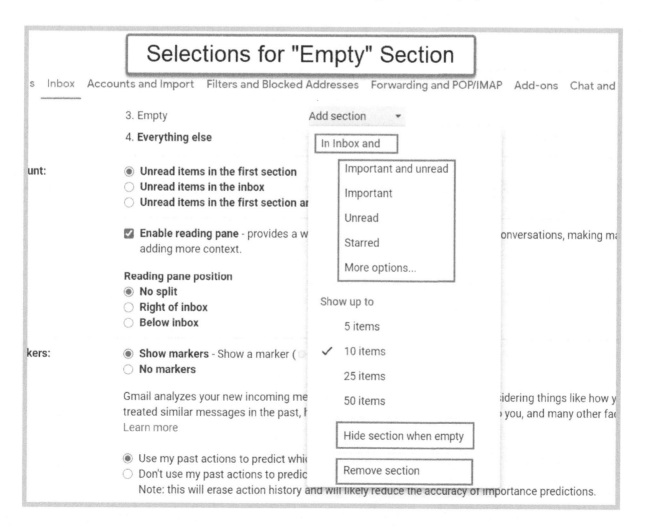

Multiple Inbox view

To select this view, go to **Gear Icon**, **See all settings**, **Inbox tab**, **Inbox type**, and click the drop-down and select **Multiple Inboxes**.

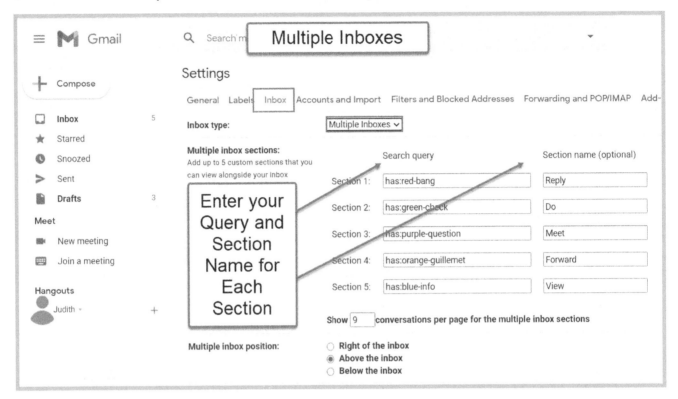

This view allows for multiple customizations. This is a more advanced feature than the others shown already. Search is discussed in detail in Appendix 2. If you are interested in using a search query-based inbox, you will want to spend some time with Appendix 2.

Changing your inbox view without leaving the Inbox

Quickly change the Inbox view from the **Quick Settings** pane. Click the **Gear Icon** to reveal **Quick Settings** and scroll down to **Inbox Type**.

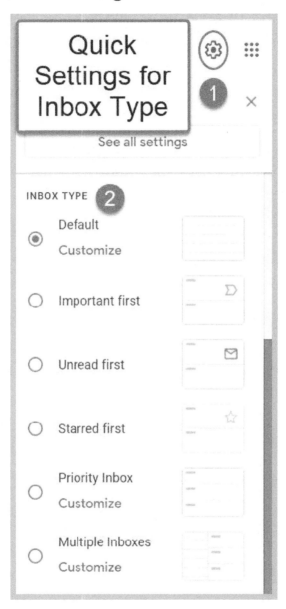

You can see the same options that you found in the Settings—Inbox tabs are now presented here, right in your Inbox. The difference here is that you can quickly switch and switch back without ever going through all the steps to go to the Settings area.

Now that you are familiar with the Settings area, let's look at your Inbox screen.

Selecting the email you want to work with

☑ If you choose the check box at the top of the screen, you will select ALL the emails on that page ONLY. You may have several pages, but you can only select them one page at a time. When we looked at Settings in the General Tab, you selected the number of emails to be shown per page: 10, 15, 20, 25, 50, or 100 per page. If you chose 50, you would see 50 per page, if you chose 100, then you will see 100 per page; you may need to scroll to the bottom of the page to see them all.

☑ If you select the box next to a specific email, you will be acting only on that one or that conversation.

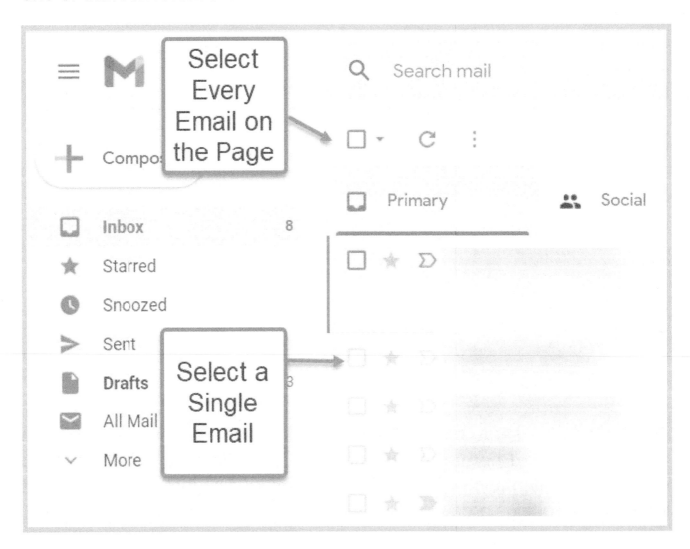

How to go between pages of the Inbox

Arrow keys on the upper right of the Inbox screen take you between Older / Newer Pages in your account.

Below you see this Gmail Account has 1,453 emails. This is the total number of emails in "All Mail." View the Oldest first or Newest first.

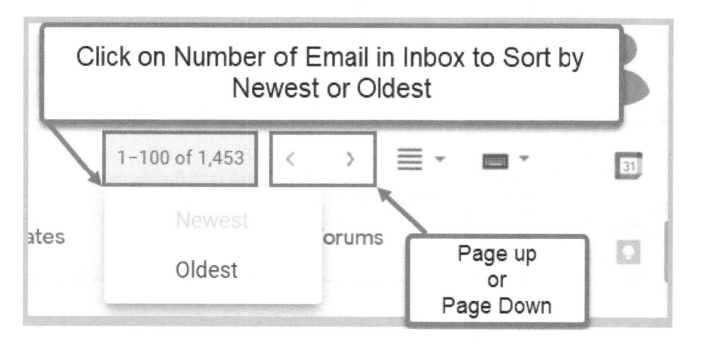

Navigation Pane

Above the **+ Compose** button are three stacked lines, often referred to as the "**Hamburger** button." Use this to expand or contract the Navigation Pane. Expanding the Navigation Pane shows the names of the categories.

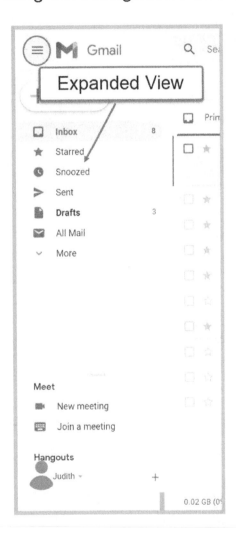
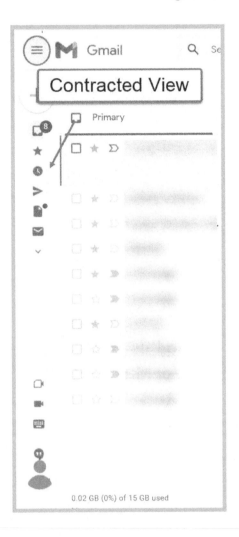

Contracting the Navigation Pane will show only the Icons. Clicking the Hamburger button to contract the Navigation Pane is great for those times you need more space for the content of the Inbox. It is especially helpful if you are using a tablet or smaller laptop.

Reading Pane

This setting will allow you to see the text of a selected email (you checked the box next to it in the list of emails) in the Inbox next to or below your list of emails.

To turn on or change the position of the Reading Pane from **Quick Settings**, click the **Gear Icon**, and scroll down to **Reading Pane**.

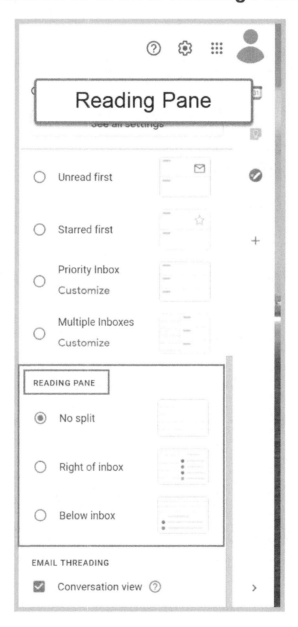

To access this in the main Settings Area, Click on the **Gear Icon**, then on **See all Settings, Inbox Tab,** then go to **Reading Pane**, check the box to enable.

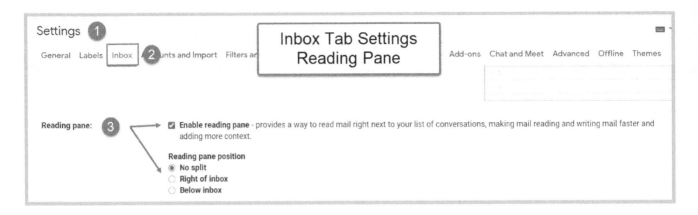

Once you turn this feature on in Settings, when you go to your Inbox, your view will show the list of emails on the left and the preview on the right (or the bottom, if that was your choice in Settings).

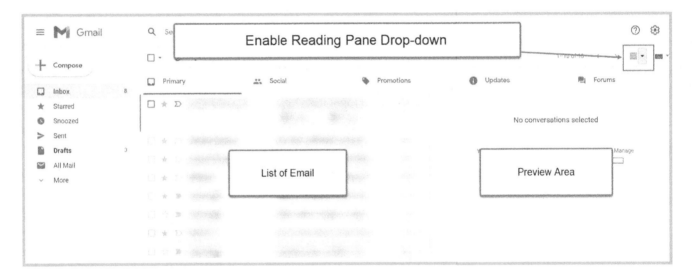

Click on the button with four horizontal lines to turn Preview on or off as desired.

Click the Down Arrow to select No split, Vertical split, or Horizontal split.

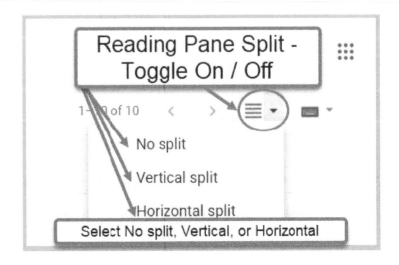

Horizontal split

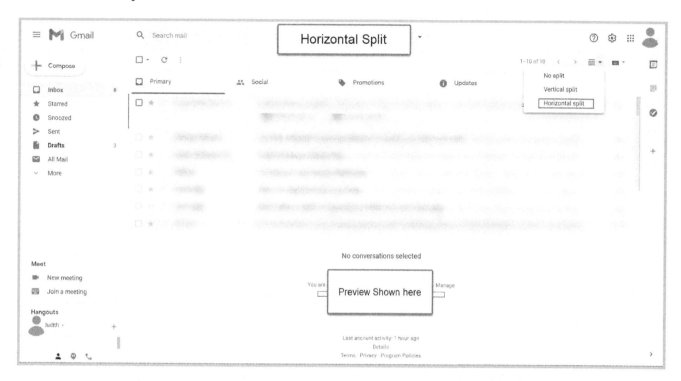

Vertical split

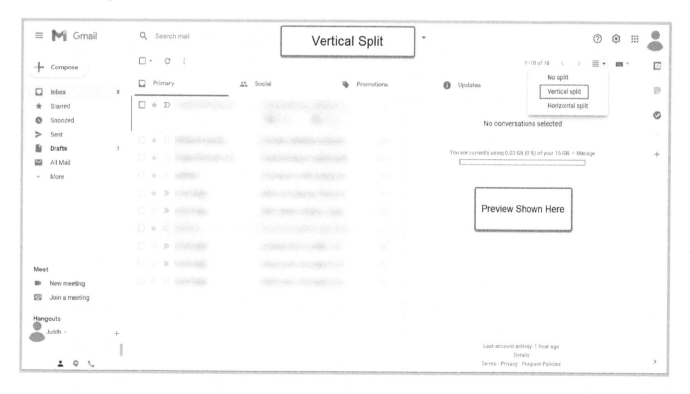

Composing an email with Gmail

To create a new message, click the **[+] Compose** button on the left-hand side of the screen.

The new message appears.

If you'd prefer it in the middle of the screen, on the top right-hand side, click the two headed diagonal arrow. This will open the box featuring larger text in the middle of the screen. This is not necessary, but it is an option for better visibility.

Address the email

In Google, your contacts are located in an App called **Google Contacts**. Go to the upper right of the screen and click on the icon that has the nine small dots, sometimes referred to as the Waffle button. Scroll down to select Contacts from the list and click on it.

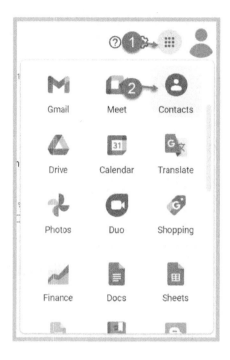

The below screen will appear after you click on Contacts. From here you can add new contacts or edit existing ones.

If you are sending email to someone already in your contacts, go to the address field and begin typing the email address of your recipient.

Since you corresponded with this person already, just typing the first few characters of their email address will show it there for you to select.

To add more recipients, hit the tab key, and enter their addresses as above. Hit the tab key to remove recipients, click the X next to their email address.

Cc (carbon copy) a recipient and/or Bcc (blind carbon copy) a recipient

A Cc shows to whom a copy of the email was sent. The person named in the blind carbon copy field will get a copy of the email, but none of the other recipients will know that this person is getting a copy of the email (use with extreme caution).

Cc or Bcc to your CRM, Evernote, or Trello accounts for project-related email

Click down and type in the subject of the email, then click inside the body.

Subject lines

Now that you have set up the Inbox with the Density you like, selected your Inbox Style, and opened and addressed an email, let's talk about Subject Lines.

The Subject Line of an email should tell the recipient what you need. When a recipient can look at the subject of an email and without ever opening it, know what it is about, you are doing it right.

This is a great time saver we can all benefit from using. When the Subject Line is clear, staff, clients, and customers are much more likely to open it, act on it, and refer to it later.

Email Subject Lines like: "Hi", "RE: your request," "About our meeting," and "Need to talk to you," are some of the most ignored Subject Lines.

Subject Lines like: "Meeting_ XYZ Corp_Milford_123121" or "VacationRequests_Q1_due_123121" are much clearer.

If the message is FYI, include that right in the Subject Line. Is it urgent? Do you need it by close of business today? Put that in the Subject Line.

The same philosophy is true for naming attachment files. Attachment file names that include the **year, subject, creator, and version** will be easy to find. Your staff will be able to locate them without having to open them and know that they have the right one.

Once you decide on your system, add it to the list of processes outlined for your business. This way, all employees can follow the company naming conventions.

Need help shaping your naming conventions? Think these four words: *Find, Act, Maintain, Explain*

- Find: How will "future you" find this email? To what is it related? Is it a proposal, company policy, request for trip reports, your expense report, or an announcement?
- Act: What do you want the recipient of the email to do?
- Maintain: Consistently use your Subject Line and Attachment naming structure.
- Explain, Enlighten, Elaborate, Express: Share information worth sharing. Respect your reader's time. Keep it short and to the point.

Format the email body text

Click and drag to highlight text, change the font, the font size, make it bold-faced, italic, underlined, change the color, or the justification, add numbers, bullets, and indent the text.

When done formatting, go to the bottom of the screen. You can do several more things with this email.

- Use the Paper Clip icon to attach a file
- Add a Hyperlink
- Add Emoji
- Insert a File from Google Drive
- Insert a photo
- Confidential Mode
- Insert Signatures
- Click on the More button (three dots) to use templates, add Labels, Print, or Check Spelling
- Trash the message

Save an email as a draft

If you start creating an email, but you need to gather more information and continue composing later, click the X on the top right-hand side of the screen to save and close it. You will find it in the **Drafts** Label. Don't worry if you forget to click the X and you close Gmail, it will automatically go to the **Drafts** Label. By default, as you work on an email, after three seconds of inactivity, your email is saved as a Draft. Clients are often surprised to find a number of Drafts in the **Drafts** Label. Usually this is the cause.

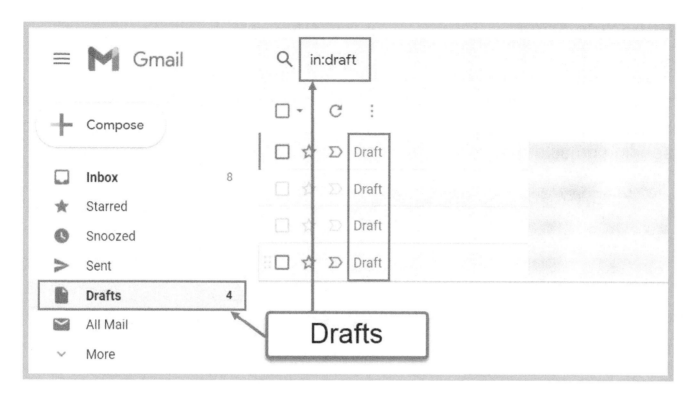

If you're completely done with this email and decide that you don't want to send it at all, hit the **Trash Can** icon on the lower right of your draft. This will discard the draft.

In our example above, the **Drafts Label** is on the left-hand side of the screen. The number shown is the number of saved drafts. Click on the label and find the draft you need. Click once on the draft message, and it will open so you can continue working.

When you are finished and ready to send it, click the blue Send button on the bottom left-hand side and your message will be sent right then.

Schedule Send

If you click the drop-down arrow to the right of the send button, you can schedule your email to send at some time in the future. **Schedule Send** is helpful if you are working late at night and don't want others seeing you are sending email at 2 a.m.

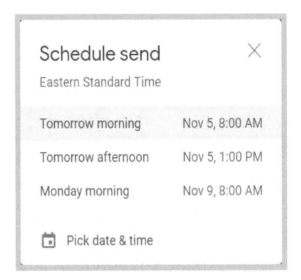

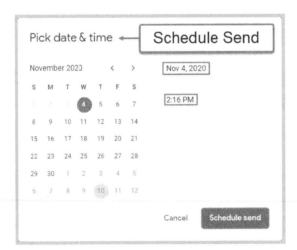

Undo Send

Have you ever hit Send on an email and wish you hadn't? Forgot to add the attachment and noticed the moment you hit Send? Not to worry, Gmail has your back. Right down at the bottom, there's an Undo button. Gmail offers you a few seconds grace period to decide if you really don't want to send that message. If that happens, just click **Undo**. You can change the number of seconds for this grace period. To do that, click the **Gear Icon** on the top right-hand side of the screen. Choose **See all settings** and go to **Settings, General Tab** and look for the **Undo Send** section.

Here's where you can choose the cancellation period. Set it for five seconds all the way up to 30 seconds.

You will see the Undo button at the bottom left for the number of seconds you selected. Click Undo and your email will not be sent.

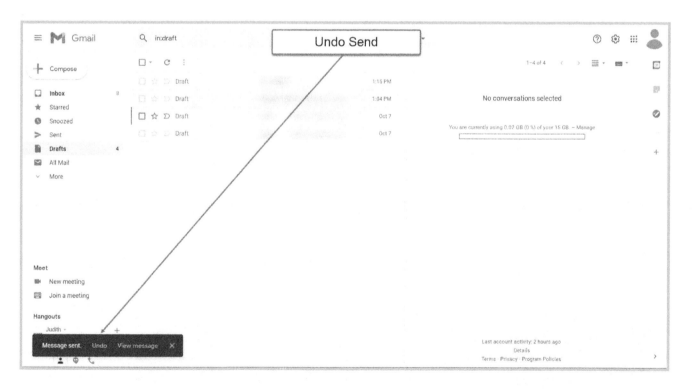

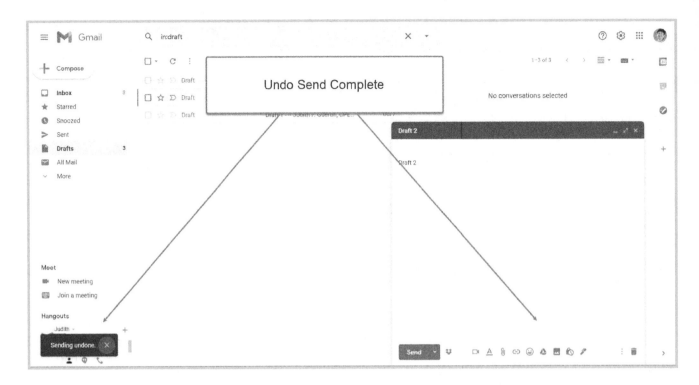

Undo Send Complete. Rewrite email or return to the Inbox list.

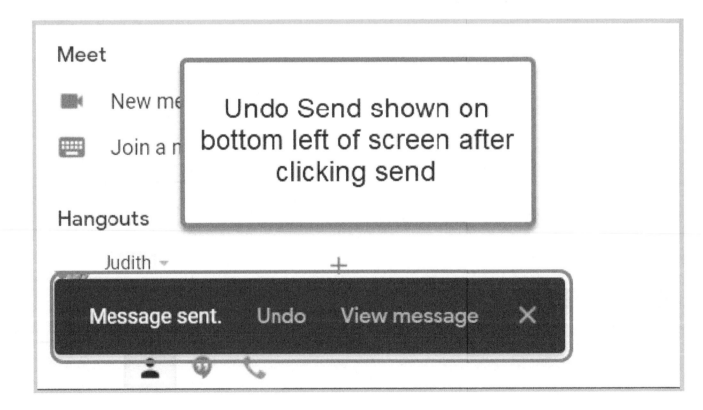

Reply to an email

The basics:

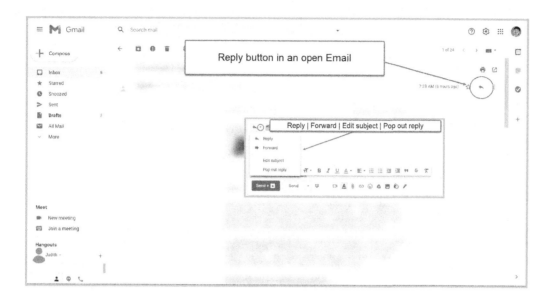

Actions available from the **More** button:

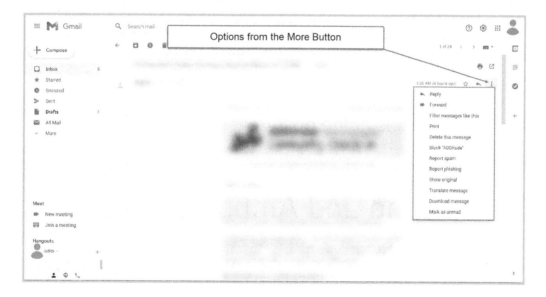

Options from drop down arrow of an email reply

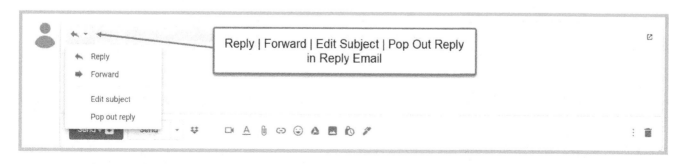

Beyond the basics: Send & Archive, Schedule Send

Go to the **Gear Icon, See all settings**, the **General** Tab and click the **Show "Send and Archive"** button in reply to make this option available.

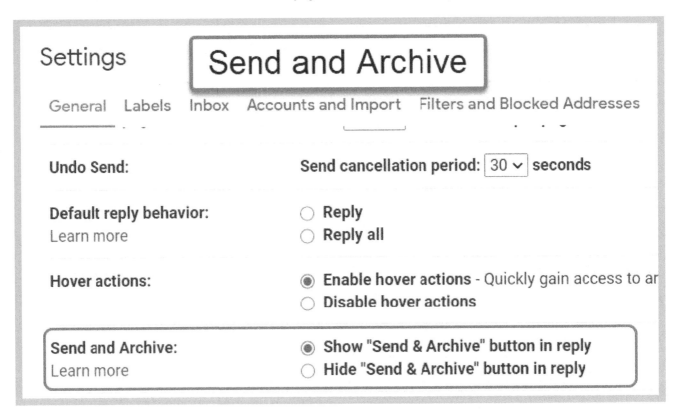

You will see these options at the bottom of the reply screen.

Schedule Send

Send & Archive and Schedule Send

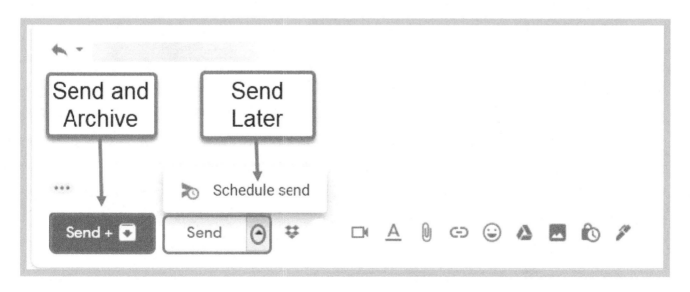

Once you select **Schedule send**, this pop out will be shown.

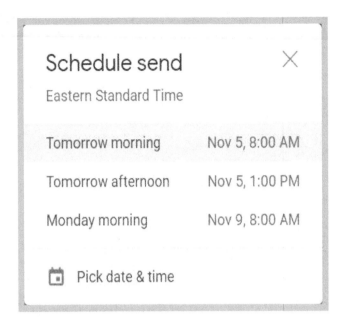

Pick from the three suggested times: Tomorrow morning, Tomorrow afternoon, or Monday morning.

The other option is to use the Pick date & time selection. Click on the Calendar Icon and pick a Month, Day, and Year. In the next screen, pick the time and click on **Schedule send**.

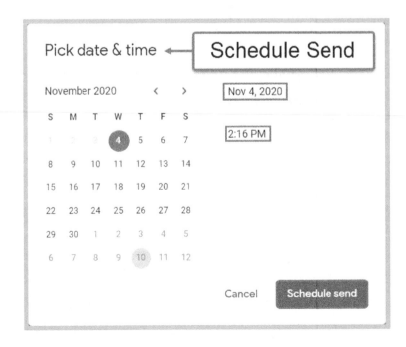

Canned responses: The power of systems

Do you find yourself answering the same questions by email daily?

Anytime you find yourself doing the same thing over and over, you need a S.Y.S.T.E.M. (Saving You Space Time Energy and Money)!

Here is an easy fix. Create Templates for repetitive responses otherwise known as "Canned Responses." Compose the Text, save as a Template, and it will be available any time you need to send a similar response. Perform any needed edits to the email populated by the Template and send the email.

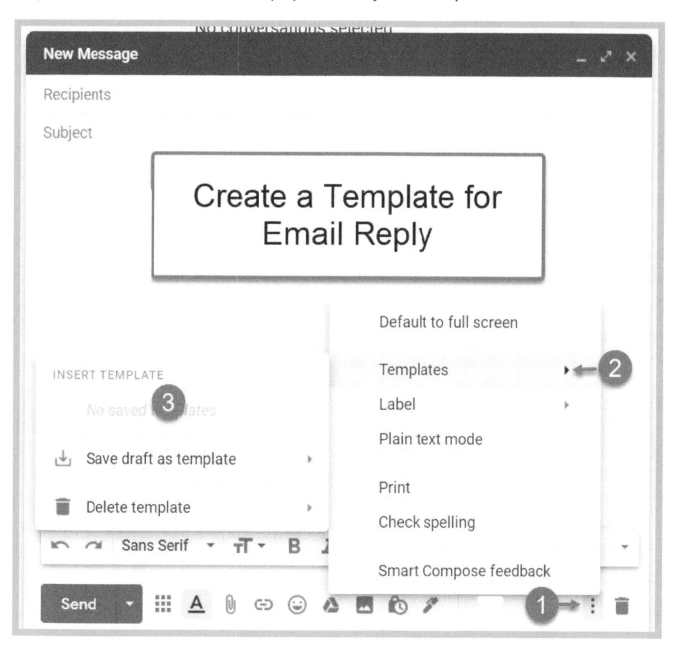

Customize the email Signature Box

Vacation Responder

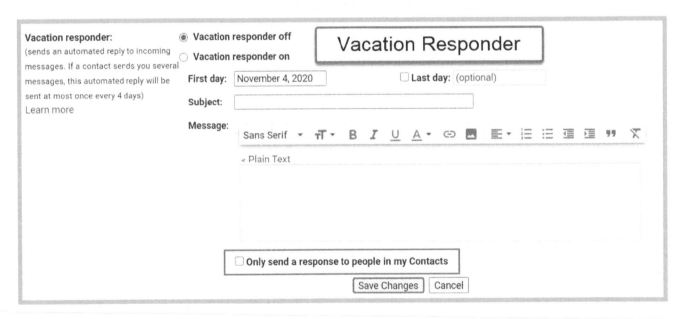

Turn this on and Gmail will send a reply to the email you receive when you are away. Select the dates then add a subject and a brief message. Check the box **Only send a response to people in my Contacts**.

5. Managing Your Inbox: Three Decisions for Success

For over 40 years, Barbara has been teaching the File, Act, Toss (FAT) system for dealing with paper clutter. Now, we will show you how to use it when dealing with your Inbox.

 THE FILE ACT TOSS SYSTEM™
(The FAT System)

> Often we look at a pile of papers—or an overflowing email inbox—and feel overwhelmed. The good news is that it's not nearly as complicated as you may imagine. There are only three decisions you can make about any document: File, Act, or Toss.

File

File is for the Email you need to save for future reference. There are two basic ways to File in Gmail: Archive or Save in a Label.

File to the Archive

There are several ways to send email to the Archive. *If you wonder where the Archive is, you have a lot of company. You will find Archived email in "All Mail."*

Find your Archive

Scroll down to All Mail in the Navigation Pane.

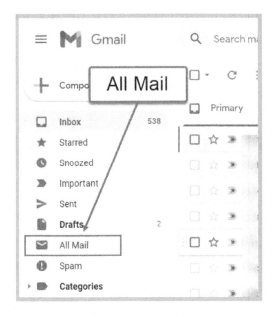

(If you do not see All Mail in your default view, click the down arrow by the word More at the bottom of the Navigation Pane.)

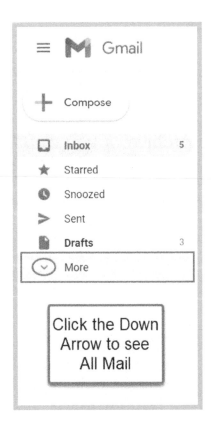

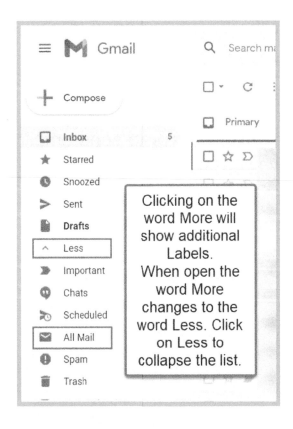

Archive: Icons view or Text view

When we looked at **Settings** earlier, we looked at Button Labels in the **General** tab. You have two choices in **Settings**, **General tab** for how these will be shown: **Icons** or **Text**.

In the **Icons View**, the Archive button looks like a bin with a down arrow. Click on this icon to send the selected emails to the archive. An info box will pop up at the bottom of the screen to tell you the email has been Archived.

Icons view

Select the check box next to the email, then click the **Archive Icon**.

Text view

Select the check box in front of an email and click the word **Archive**.

Another way to the Archive is to hover your mouse over an email in the list until you **see the icons appear**. Click on the **Archive** Icon. Note that this option is not available if you changed to the **Text View** instead of **Icons View**.

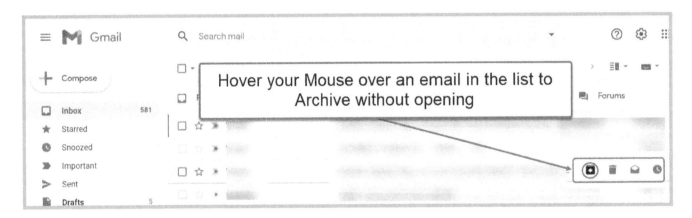

If you do not see these Icons when using the mouse to hover over the email list, go to the General tab in Settings to turn this feature on.

| Hover actions: | ● **Enable hover actions** - Quickly gain access to archive, delete, mark as read, and snooze controls on hover. |
| | ○ **Disable hover actions** |

To send an open email to the **Archive**, click the archive button above the inbox as shown below.

Use the Keyboard Shortcut to **Archive.**

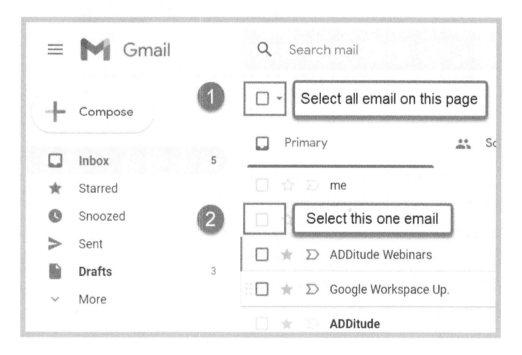

We will discuss Keyboard Shortcuts in some detail in Appendix 1, but this one is so good, I will share it with you now.

Select the email you wish to Archive. Select the check box at the top of the page to select all email on that page or select the boxes next to the individual emails you wish to archive. Yes, you can check more than one box on a page, even if they are not next to one another. Now hit the "e" key on the keyboard. Yes, that is all you have to do. All those emails will be archived to All Mail. How easy is that?

If you Archive an email or emails in error, click the **Undo** button at the bottom of the screen, and the email will return to the Inbox.

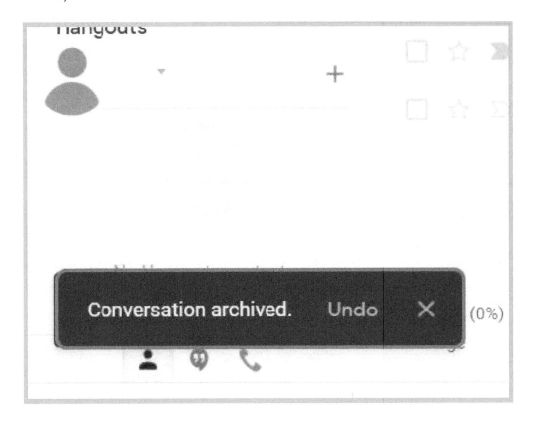

File it with Important Marker, Star, or a Label

Rather than creating Folders in the Gmail system, you group emails together by creating Labels. The maximum number of labels you can create in Gmail is 5,000, which includes sub-labels. The emails will be searchable by their assigned labels. Assign multiple labels to the same email if needed.

Another option is to move emails from the Inbox and store them by their labels. Once stored by their label, they will no longer show in the Inbox. To view them, click on the Label, or use the Search Box. Create as many labels as you need; delete them when you no longer need to view these emails sorted in this manner. In the following example, I created a Label for Gmail from Google called **Google**. Search for this label with the term **label:google** in the Search box. The Google label is highlighted in the Navigation Pane view below.

Clicking on the Label in the **Navigation Pane** will show a list of all matching emails.

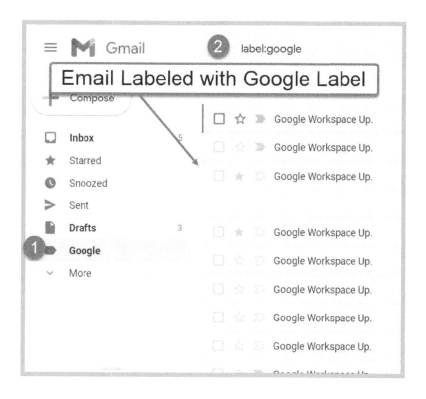

Important Markers

The Important Marker is the Yellow right pointing arrow in the illustration below. Adding the Important Marker will help train Gmail what senders are important to you.

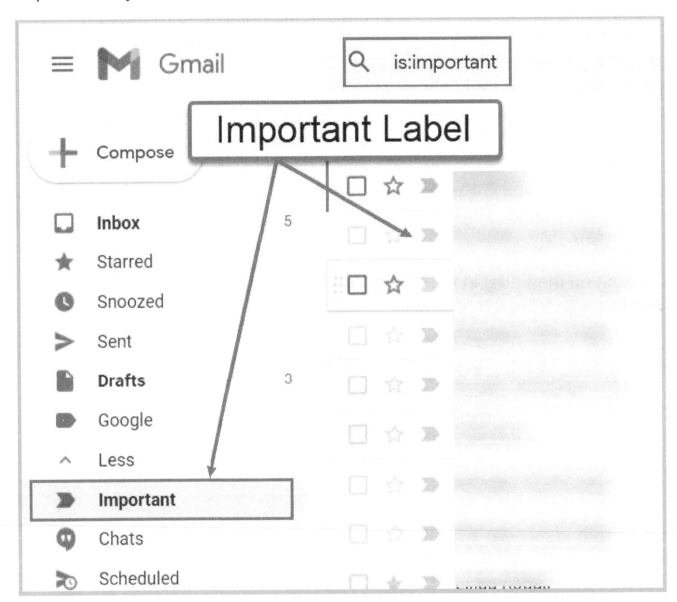

Stars

Add Stars to your filing/finding system to distinguish importance or next actions. Find them in **Settings**, **General Tab**, scroll down to **Stars**. You are free to use all, some, or none of them.

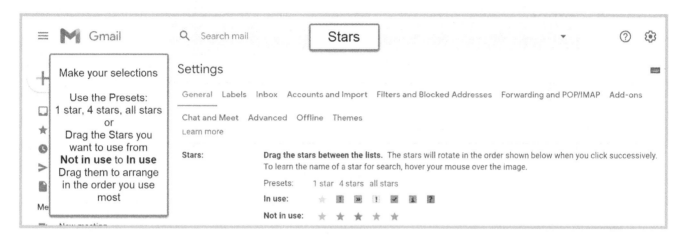

Stars all have names which you cannot change. If you are a visual person and color helps you, using stars may be an option. By default, Google gives you the "1-star" option, which is the **yellow-star**. You search for items with it by typing "has:" and the name of the star. For example, "has:**yellow-star**."

You will need to remember what you use each star to represent. For example, the **green-check** might mean you completed the action associated with this email. The **purple-question** might show something you need to research, and you can use the exclamation point (called **yellow-bang** in this star system) for things that need attention today. Use what works for you.

To select the proper star in a message, click on the **Star** (next to the check box) in the list of emails by clicking successively on the **Star** until you see the one you need. Each click will take you to the next one on the list. Only the stars you moved to the '**In use**' area will be available here.

To add other Stars to choose from, go back to **Settings** and drag them to "**In use**."

Below is a list of all the Star names to use for search. (You will only see the Stars you selected in Settings.) Notice, in these names, there are no spaces, and each star name has a dash between the words. You will need to type this into the Search Box with this exact structure.

- yellow-star
- orange-star
- red-star
- purple-star
- blue-star
- green-star

- red-bang
- orange-guillemet
- yellow-bang
- green-check
- blue-info
- purple-question

Notice the selections in the "In use" section is different in the boxes below.

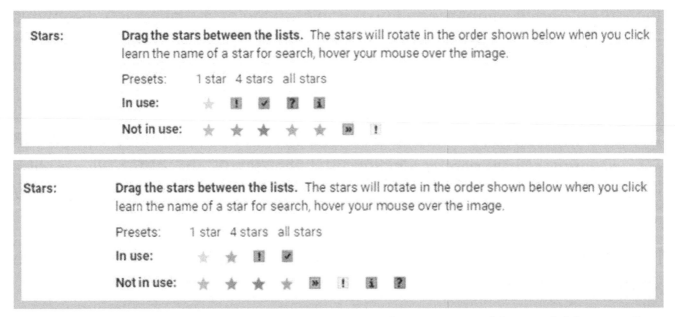

Add as many or as few as you like or use the presets "1 star," "4 stars," or "all stars." It is really up to you. Just be sure they are meaningful in your system, otherwise they are simply more clutter.

Labels

If you are a PC user, you are no doubt familiar with Folders. You create them, name them, and put files in them. If you delete the Folder, you delete everything in it. Well, in Gmail, we have Labels, not Folders.

Folders and Labels are two different animals. Labels are more like Tags. We use Tags in many other productivity tools. For example, you may be familiar with Evernote. Add as many tags as you want to a note to help you find it later based on the name of the Tag. Labels in Gmail work much the same way. It is a system for grouping email together, to make them easier to find later. Unlike deleting a traditional PC Folder where deleting the Folder deletes the Folder and everything in it, deleting a Label will NOT delete the email, it only deletes the Label. You will no longer be able to sort by that Label. The emails are still in your account. You will find them in the "All Mail" Label.

You can even add multiple labels to one email. This allows you to search by different terms, which can be helpful. Add one Label with the name of a person, another for the name of a project, another for the name of the event. You may add as many as you need to add context for searching later.

Labels are shown in the Navigation Pane. From here, you can check what email uses a particular Label, delete Labels that are no longer needed, or create new ones.

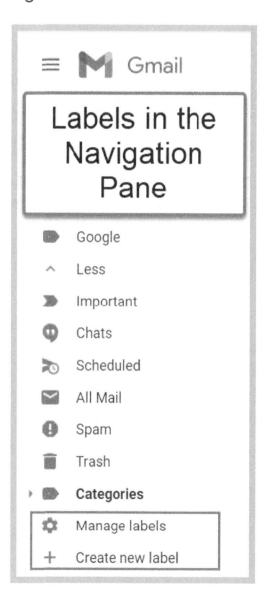

Assign a color to different labels

Visual learners love color. Here is one more way Gmail lets you use the rainbow in your system. Color your Labels to add another context. For example: use a green label for emails related to finance, orange for emails related to work, and blue for emails related to business.

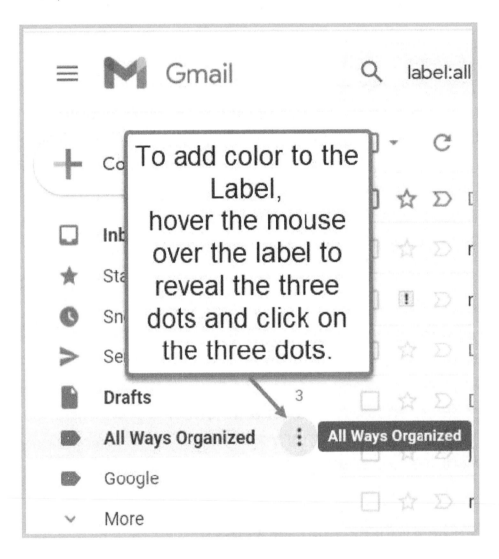

When you click on the three dots, a pop-out appears.

Make your selections.

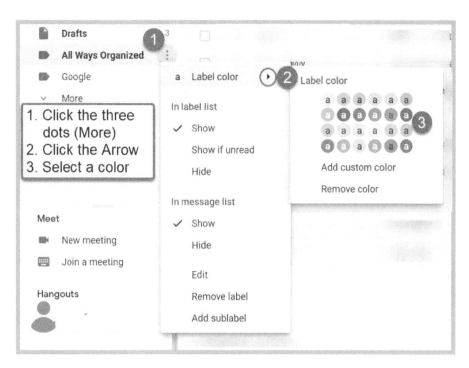

In addition to adding color, you can set up a filter to apply the Label to messages as they arrive from that sender. They will really POP in your Inbox. Use them only for your most important, can't miss email.

A new screen opens where you create the filter. The sender of the email you selected will be shown here in the From field.

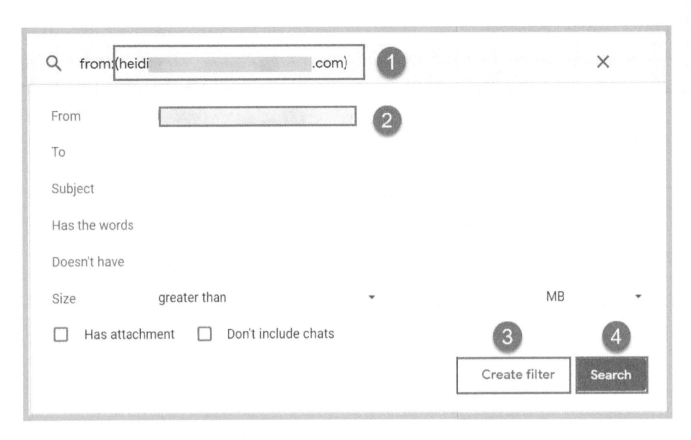

Click **Create Filter** and the screen below appears. Check the box **Apply the label** and choose the label from the list and click **Create filter**.

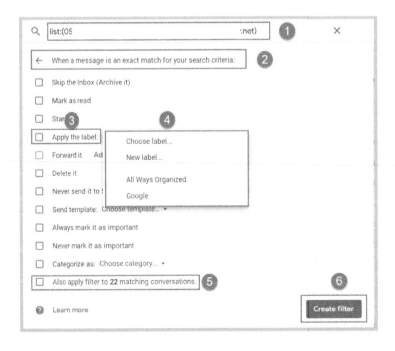

Here is the result of the orange colored label with the filter applied to a new message that arrived in the Inbox.

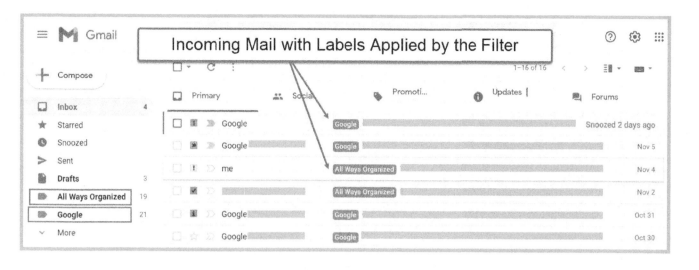

Create and manage labels in Settings—Labels Tab

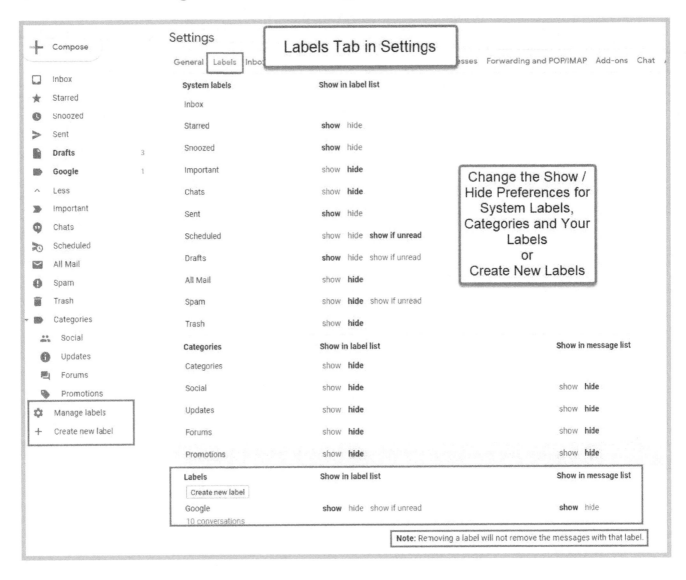

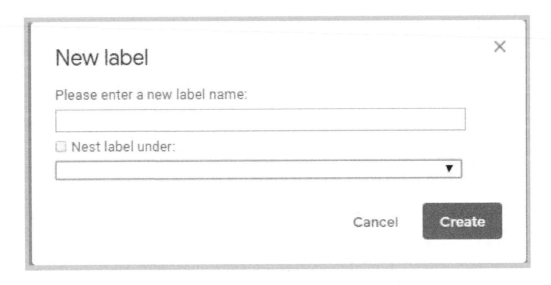

Searching by label

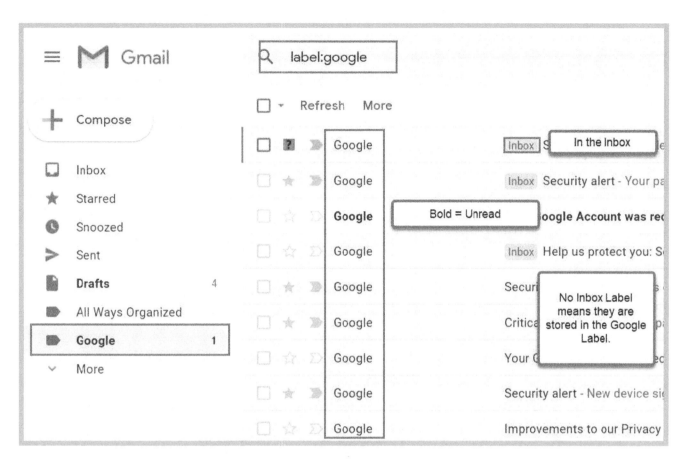

The emails in this group are all assigned the **Google** Label. To view the email in the Google Label, select the Google Label from the **Navigation Pane** or use the search box and type in **label:google**.

Create rules to filter your emails

Use filters to keep reference-only material out of your Inbox. Instead, use a filter to send them to a designated label, skipping the Inbox first.

Imagine, for example, there are newsletters you receive that are clogging your Inbox. They might be fun to read when you have time, but you don't want them to distract you from actionable items in your Inbox. You can filter messages like these to go to a Label called Fun Reading, Newsletters, or something that will tell you the contents of the Label. When you have time to read them, click the Label and there they are, ready to be read.

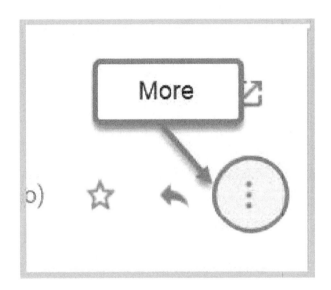

- Open Gmail
- Open an email
- Click More on upper right
- Click Filter messages like these
- Enter your filter criteria
- Click Create filter
- Click on the More button

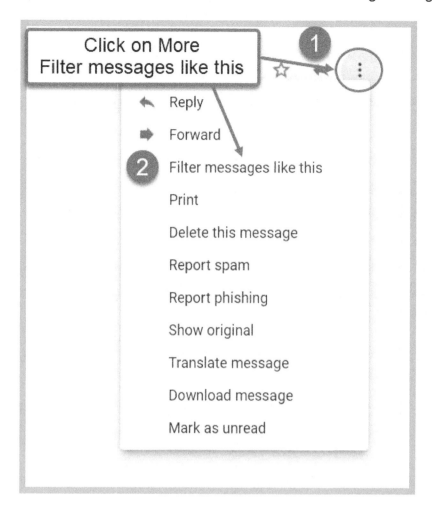

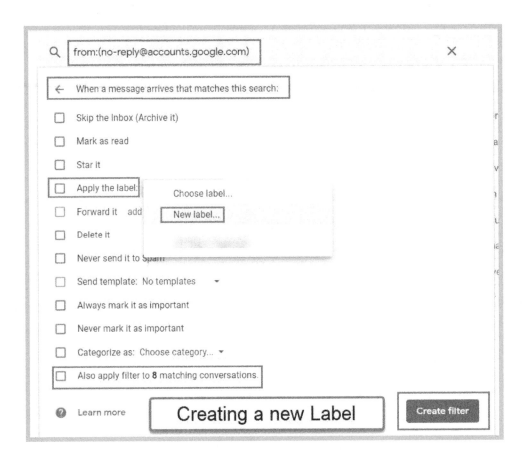

Creating a new Label

Once you create the new **Label** you can apply it to the matching email in your Inbox by checking the box next to: **Also apply filter to _ matching conversations.**

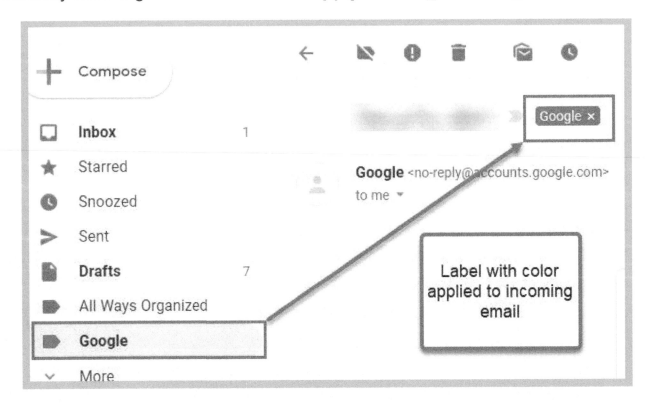

Label with color applied to incoming email

Act

What is your next action with the remaining email?

- Reply: Answer the sender's email
- Reply All: Send a reply to all addressees of this message
- Forward: Send this message to someone else not named in the original To field
- Send to programs outside Gmail: Evernote, Trello, Asana among others
- Save the Attachments: Send the attachments to Google Drive, Dropbox, Box, and others
- Create an Event
- Create a Task
- Create a Note
- Snooze: Schedule the email to return to the top of the Inbox when you choose to deal with it

Snooze

In Gmail, you have the option to **Snooze** an email. When you open an email, and you know you will not deal with it until later, choose the **Snooze Label.**

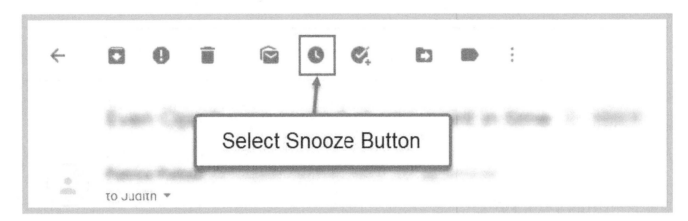

It will remove this item from your Inbox temporarily and deliver it again at the day and time you select.

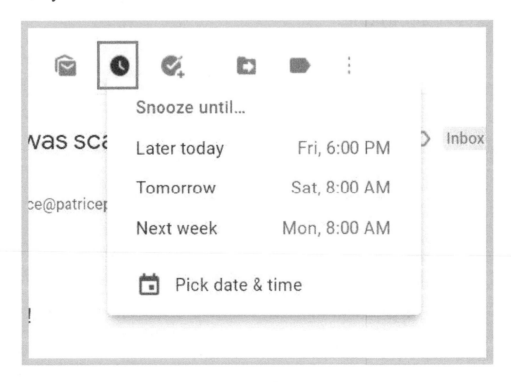

This is the digital equivalent of the Tickler file we use for our paper files in the Productive Environment System.™ Files are saved to the month and day we choose. The Snoozed emails will return to the top of Inbox on the assigned date. When it returns to the Inbox, there is a notation to the right of the Subject Line about when it was Snoozed.

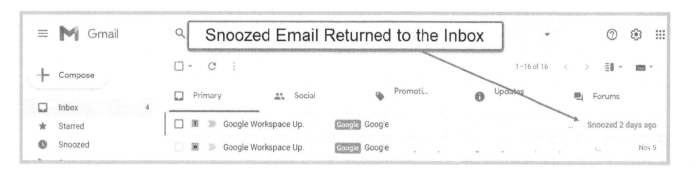

It is a bit of magic! Does this concern you? Fear not! If you need to see this email before the snooze date, go to the **Snoozed Label** on the **Navigation Pane**, or type **in:snoozed** in the **Search Box** and all your snoozed emails will be there waiting for you. Try it, you will love it!

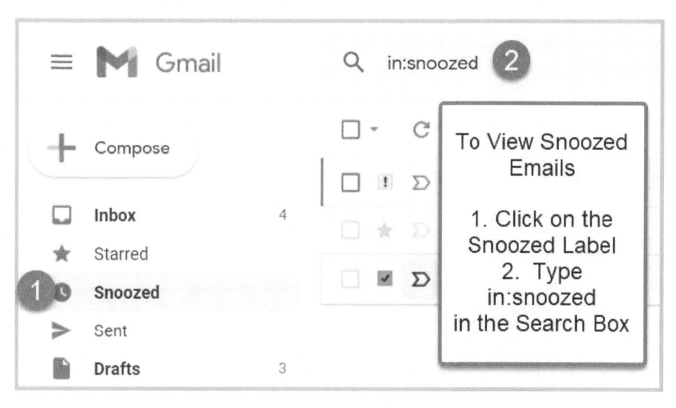

Send to a program outside Gmail

Connect to cloud accounts like Box or Drop Box

Click on the + in the side bar and select the application you want to add from the available applications. Follow the instructions in the pop out.

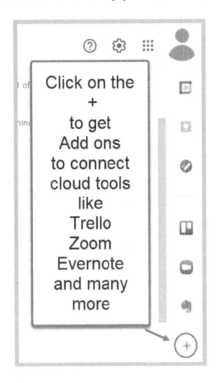

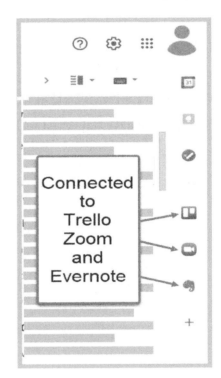

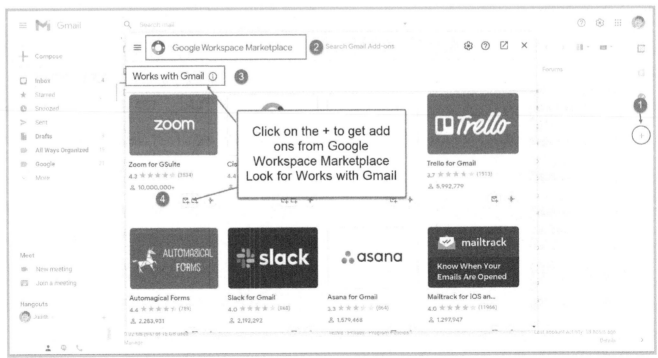

Save conversations as PDFs in your Google Drive

Search for emails you want to save. For example: search for all invoices. Perform search, select the appropriate emails then, click on the Printer Icon at the upper right.

From the Printer set-up page, select **Save to PDF** or **Save to Google Drive**.

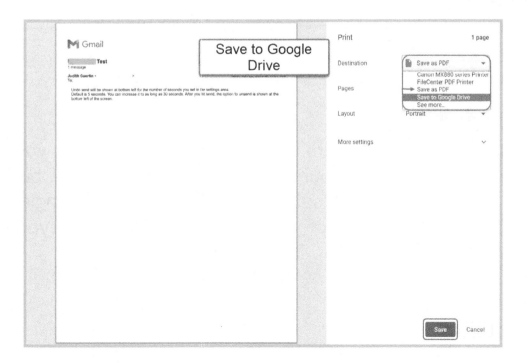

Save only the attachments

Open the email, hover over the attachment, and select the Google Drive Icon.

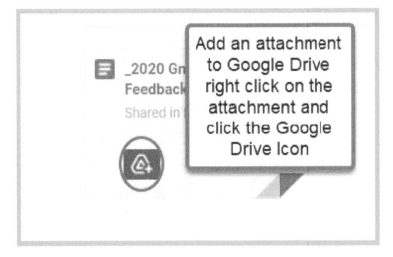

Save multiple attachments to Google Drive

With one click, open the email, scroll to the bottom, and click on the Google Drive Icon just above the attachments.

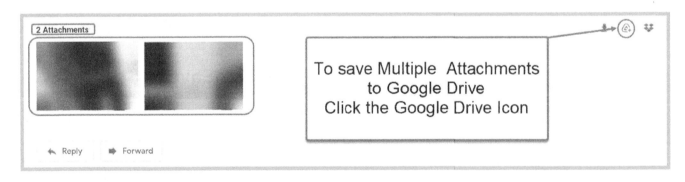

Click **Organize** to select where to save the attachments in your Google Drive. If you miss this step, your files will be in Google Drive, but they will not be in a specific Folder. You can move them inside Google Drive by dragging them to the Folder of your choice. (Unlike Gmail, you do have Folders in Google Drive.)

The More button

The More button (the three dots) at the top right of an email will give you multiple options to choose from in addition to Reply and Forward. You can: Filter messages like this, Print, Delete this message, Block a sender, Report spam, Report phishing, Show original, Translate, Download, or Mark as unread.

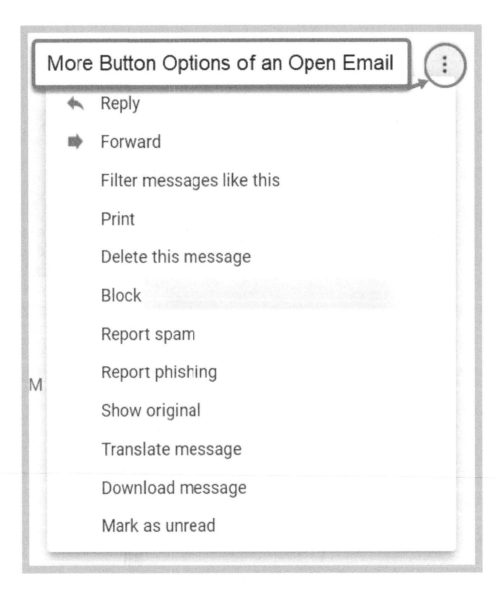

Toss

Send to the Trash label

Toss is for the emails you no longer need. Send them to the **Trash Label** by clicking the **Trash Can Icon**. *Note that by default Gmail sent to the Trash Label remains there for 30 days, then they are permanently deleted.

It is good to know that if you perform this action by accident, you can go to the Trash and return the email in question to your Inbox.

If you need to free space on your drive, go to the Trash Label and empty the deleted items. The space you clear is added back to your account. If you don't want to take this extra step, wait the 30 days for the deleted items to be removed automatically, and the storage space will be returned.

Unsubscribe

If you want less email in your Inbox, Unsubscribe is your new best friend. Without all that clutter, you can go straight to the messages that matter!

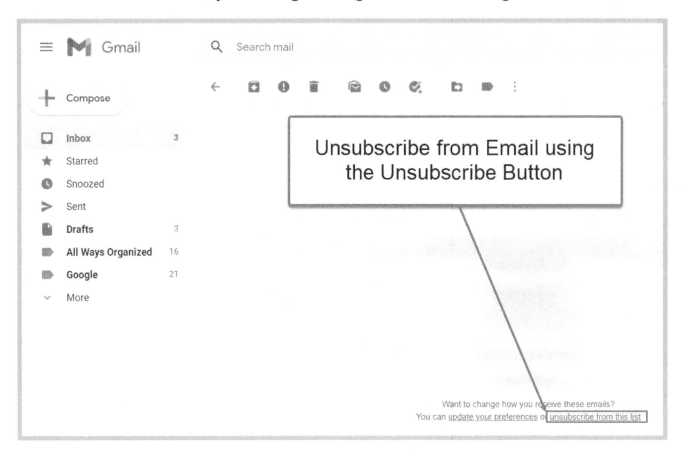

Don't feel you need to give up all your subscriptions. Keep the best and get rid of the rest. It is OK to unsubscribe from email you no longer want.

If you don't feel ready to unsubscribe from all your subscriptions just yet, start by creating a filter to put these emails in a Label. Call the Label: Newsletters, Do I Need This, Unsubscribe, or whatever makes sense to you. Configure this filter to skip the Inbox and place the email in that Label. You can find them in the Label if you need them, but they will not be in your Inbox vying for your attention. If you find you don't miss the email you filtered, you can safely unsubscribe.

Spam

If you find Spam Email in your Inbox, you can help Gmail send them the Spam label in the future by Marking them as Spam.

From an open email click the three dots (the More button) at the upper right and this pop out will appear. From here you can report the email as spam, block the sender, and delete the message.

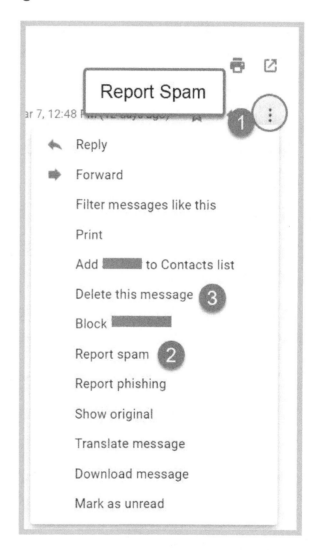

Clear out spam

Open the **Spam Label** on a regular basis to scan for mail that is not spam but may have been marked as Spam by the algorithm and mark it as "not spam." When all that remains is actual Spam, empty the **Spam Label**.

This covers the basics of sending email and File, Act, Toss. Now you are ready to deal with the Tiger's Den—your Inbox. Don't be scared, let's do this!

6. Maintenance

Getting and staying organized in any area of your life requires time and effort. Regular maintenance is necessary to keep the Tiger at bay. The good news is you now have tools to help you do just that: The Productive Environment Five Step Process™, The FAT System™ (File Act Toss), and the steps for processing your Inbox. Now, any time you need to, you can follow these simple steps to bring your inbox back under control. Next, I have a few more ways to help you maintain a Productive Environment in your Inbox!

A potpourri of other assorted Tiger Tamers

- Pin your Inbox to the Bookmarks bar of your Browser. Want to check email? Click the bookmark and go right to your Inbox.
- Turn Off Notifications! Instead of having constant notifications of new email, schedule specific times in the day to PROCESS email. Focus on your work without rings and dings! Try turning notifications off, even if only for brief periods, to allow for FOCUSED work.
- Decrease checking frequency by at least half. For example: instead of every 30 minutes, check hourly. Congratulate yourself on taking baby steps.
- Stop staring at your Inbox, waiting for a response. Do you assume your customers and colleagues are waiting for an instant response to their email? Your behavior with your own Inbox will train others how you deal with email. If you always answer in seconds, then those you correspond with will come to expect an instant response.
- Set the expectation for less frequent checking, then create an email signature stating when you will check email. Note in your email signature that you check at 10 a.m. and 4 p.m. (or whatever times work in your day) to let recipients know not to expect an instant answer.
- Go to Settings, General Tab, and create an email signature. This information will be automatically added to your outgoing emails.

- Tell them how to reach you if the matter is urgent. Provide an alternate
- method of reaching you in that same signature: "If you require immediate attention, call xxx-xxx-xxxx." If you prefer text messages, you can indicate that as well.
- Do not answer email during non-office hours. If you must reply during non-office time, schedule the email you wrote at 2 a.m. to be sent at 9 a.m. the next day, during normal business hours.
- Again, you are setting expectations. If you show others you are always working, they will want access when you should be having family time or time just for yourself. You deserve to enjoy your evenings, weekends, and vacations too!
- Connect other programs from within your email client if at all possible. Use Zoom Meeting and Free Conference Call Add-ons. Save items to Cloud Storage services like Box, Dropbox, or Google Drive. Check if your CRM (Customer Relationship Manager) has a Side Panel tool available for you to add to the Gmail Side Panel.
- Don't forget that the Side Panel also includes a button to open your Tasks, a Google Keep note, or your Google Calendar. So easy to check your Calendar if you need to schedule an appointment, make a note, or add a task and not need to leave your Inbox.

Stop Inbox overload: What about Inbox Zero?

- Inbox Zero is not the reality for most of us. What most people are trying to achieve is an Inbox where all items are seen on one screen with white space at the bottom of the Inbox.
- Use Guy Kawasaki's Five Sentence (or fewer) Email. Why five sentences or less? Long emails are either unread, or if they are read, they are not answered. Fewer than five sentences can seem abrupt. Remember, the purpose of email is to have the recipient take some sort of action.
- Evaluate your relationship with the **Promotions** and **Social Tabs**: Empty them regularly and consider a recurring calendar entry to prompt decluttering your subscriptions. The surest way to keep your Inbox clear is to keep meaningless things from entering your email.
- Clear Out **Spam**. Check on a regular basis to scan for actual mail that is not spam and mark it as "not spam."

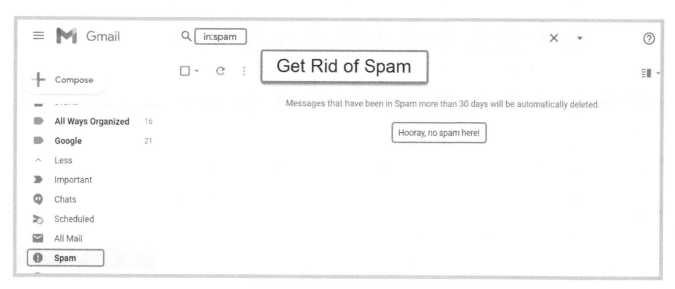

Reminder: Tech Is constantly changing

We have made every effort to show you the most updated version of Gmail. In the tech world, software is constantly changing. There were some updates that occurred as we were writing this book, necessitating updates to the manuscript even as we were preparing for publication.

You can expect that Gmail, and all Google Software (or any software for that matter) will be upgraded and features may be added, changed, or removed periodically. This is especially true of the Experimental Access features you may have enabled in Settings. Some go on to become part of Gmail, and others will disappear, never to be seen again. I think you can safely say that the key features you have come to depend upon will remain part of Gmail. You just may need to search the Settings area to find them.

There you have it, the basics of Gmail. It's a lot to think about and configure for your business.

Remember, it is a productivity buffet. Take what you want and leave the rest. If you are still hungry for more you can come back for a second or third helping.

If you are the kind of person who is ready to implement what you read here, Barbara and I are already cheering for you!

If you need some guidance, support, or coaching, we are here for you. Lots of our clients learn best by working with us side by side. We are ready to help you:

- Learn how to set up and use Gmail at a higher level.
- Get answers to your specific questions.
- Customize your Inbox, your labels, the use of colors, linking to other Google tools, and tools outside of Google.
- Dive deep into customizations.
- Create your vision, understand and eliminate your obstacles, commit the right resources, create your plan, and most of all sustain your success.

Need a one-to-one coach? We can help.

Write to *judy@allwaysorganizedmass.com* to arrange for a complimentary discovery session to discuss how we can work together to take you to the next level with your Gmail account.

Ready to clear the backlog? Remember: "Clutter is Postponed Decisions®."

Prospects often ask me, "How much is this going to cost, and how long will it take?" My answer is that I can't tell you, because I don't know exactly what you need, but I can tell you one thing for sure: the longer you wait, the longer it will take and the more it will cost in lost opportunities.

I wish you all enormous success as you Tame the Digital Tiger. May you all experience ever growing productivity and profitability!

Appendix 1

Keyboard shortcuts

Want to create email faster using keyboard shortcuts? There are over 130 shortcuts you can use! Go to the **Settings** in Gmail > **General Tab**, scroll down to **Keyboard Shortcuts** and click **Turn on**, then scroll to the bottom of the page, and click the **Save Changes** button. If you decide keyboard shortcuts are not for you, come back to this area in settings and turn Keyboard Shortcuts off, scroll to the bottom and click the Save Changes button and you are back to the default setting with no keyboard shortcuts.

Note: These shortcuts won't work unless keyboard shortcuts are turned on in settings. To see a complete list of keyboard shortcuts, including which need to be turned on, type ? when you have Gmail open. Note: Keyboard shortcuts work differently on PC and Mac computers. On a PC press Ctrl and on a Mac press ⌘ and the shortcut key listed below for the action you wish to complete.

Action	Shortcut
Move focus to toolbar	,
Select conversation	x
Toggle star/rotate among stars	s
Archive	e
Mute conversation	m
Report as spam	!
Delete	#

Reply	r
Reply in a new window	Shift + r
Reply all	a
Reply all in a new window	Shift + a
Forward	f
Forward in a new window	Shift + f
Update conversation	Shift + n
Archive conversation and go previous/next	] or [
Undo last action	z
Mark as read	Shift + i
Mark as unread	Shift + u
Mark unread from the selected message	_
Mark as important	+ or =

Mark as not important	-
Expand entire conversation	;
Collapse entire conversation	:
Add conversation to Tasks	Shift + t

For a complete list, <u>visit</u> support at Google.com

No need to learn them all at once, just pick a couple and get started. Here are a few that I love.

Want to send a new email from your Gmail account?

- Press the C key, and a new email is ready to populate.

Want to zip through your messages quickly?

- Use the J key to go to the next message in the list.

Need to send a quick reply?

- Mac Command key + R
- PC Shift key + R

Want to Set Preview Pane?

- Go to Settings, Advanced Tab and click on Enable.

Auto advance to the next email in your Inbox:

- Go to **Settings** > **Advanced tab** > scroll down to **Auto-advance**. Click **Enable**.

Appendix 2

Harness the power of

Operators

Learning multiple ways to use SEARCH is a valuable skill. Effective search will show you related email that you can deal with as a group. Add labels, stars, important markers in a few clicks. Click on All Mail and use the Search Box at the top of the page.

The following chart shows numerous operators—terms with a colon following them—that help you search. For example, from:Sally, to:Barbara, subject:Retreat. Typing these operators into the Search Box of your Gmail Inbox will show you emails matching your criteria. Another example is searching: Search by size to reduce the size of your Inbox. You might search for files larger than 10M in this case. Look for files that have large attachments and save the attachments somewhere other than your email. Searching for a period of time before or after a certain date is another example. Other operators let you search by sender, something in the subject line, certain kinds of attachments, labels, by importance, by stars, email containing an exact quote, sent by a certain person, from a mailing list, and more.

These are tremendously helpful with dealing with the backlog. Search for all before a certain date and perform File, Act, Toss. Archive the ones you need to keep, and they will remain in All Mail.

Tip: Once you perform a search using search operators, you can use the results to create a filter for these messages.

What you can search	Operator	Example
Specify the sender	from:	Example: from:Barbara
Specify a recipient	to:	Example: to:Barbara
Specify a recipient who received a copy	cc: bcc:	Example: cc:Barbara Example: bcc:Judy

Words in the Subject Line	subject:	Example: subject:homework
Messages that match multiple terms	OR or { }	Example: from:Judy OR from:Barbara Example: {from:judy from:barbara}
Remove messages from your results	-	Example: dinner-drinks
Find messages with words near each other. Use the number to say how many words apart the words can be	Add quotes to find messages in which the word you put first stays first. AROUND	Example: holiday AROUND 10 retreat Example: "secret AROUND 25 party"
Messages that have a certain label	label:	Example: label:work
Messages that have an attachment	has:attachment	Example: has:attachment
Messages that have a Google Drive, Docs, Sheets, or Slides attachment or link	has:drive has:document has:spreadsheet has:presentation	Example: has:drive
Messages that have a YouTube video	has:youtube	Example: has:youtube
Messages from a mailing list	list:	Example: list:info@example.com
Attachments with a certain name or file type	filename:	Example: filename:pdf Example: filename:coursework.txt
Search for an exact word or phrase	" "	Example: "productivity power up"

Group multiple search terms together	( )	Example: subject:(mastermind retreat)
Messages in any label, including Spam and Trash	in: anywhere	Example: in: anywhere retreat
Search for messages that are marked as important	is:important label:important	Example: is:important
Starred, snoozed, unread, or read messages	is:starred is:snoozed is:unread is:read	Example: is:read is:starred
Messages that include an icon of a certain color	has:yellow-star has blue-info	Example: has:yellow-star
Recipients in the cc or bcc field	cc: bcc:	Example: cc:judy

Note: You can't find messages that you received on bcc.

Search for messages sent during a certain time period	after: before: older: newer:	Example: after:2019/05/20 Example: after:05/20/2019 Example: before:2019/05/28 Example: before:05/28/2019
Search for messages older or newer than a time period using d (day), m (month), and y (year)	older_than: newer_than:	Example: newer_than:2d
Chat messages	is:chat	Example: is:chat homework
Search by email for delivered messages	deliveredto:	Example: deliveredto:username@ example.com

Messages in a certain category	category:primary category:social category:promotions category:updates category:forums category:reservations category:purchases	Example: category:promotions category:primary
Messages larger than a certain size in bytes	size:	Example: size:1000000
Messages larger or smaller than a certain size in bytes	larger: smaller:	Example: larger:10M
Results that match a word exactly	+	Example: +jellyfish
Messages with a certain message-id header	Abc456lgid:27643	Example: Abc456lgid:27643:9232456 @example.com
Messages that have or don't have a label	has:userlabels has:nouserlabels	Example: has:nouserlabels

Note: Labels are only added to a message, not an entire conversation.

Note: When using numbers as part of your search query, a space or a dash (-) will separate a number while a dot (.) will be a decimal. For example, 01.2047-100 is considered 2 numbers: 01.2047 and 100.

Appendix 3

Google Calendar Integration

View and schedule Google Calendar appointments without leaving your Inbox

This is a great feature for checking your availability for an appointment request you received in an email or for viewing your appointments for the day. Schedule right from this window in Gmail.

Open the side panel and click on the Google Calendar Icon.

The date selected will pop out to the side showing details for the appointments on this date.

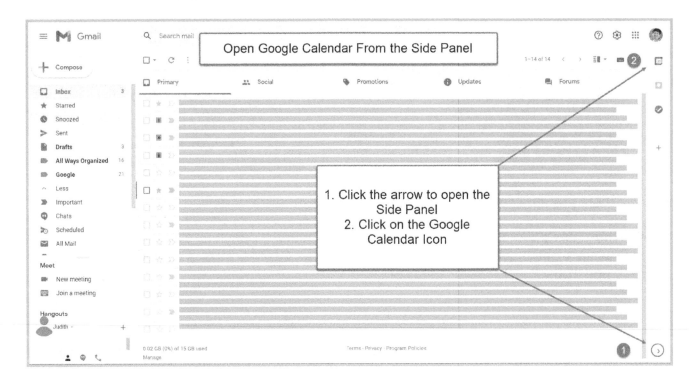

Looking at other dates in Google Calendar

1. Click on the Calendar Icon
2. Select the Date from the drop-down calendar
3. Select a date by clicking on the number
4. Use the arrows to go forward or back by months
5. Use pop our window to view full Google Calendar Page in a New Tab

If you need to see the entire calendar, click on the pop-out icon (5) and view full screen in a new tab.

Appendix 4

Google Keep integration

If you are not familiar with Google Keep, it is a simple note taking app. It is an app that is easy to share. I know many couples who use it for shared shopping lists or reminders for one another. The notes can be pinned to the top of the list for easy retrieval. Easy to find the grocery list if you keep it pinned to the top of the list! Teachers use it for keeping class assignments together in lists grouped by day of the week. You can add color or photos to any of the notes to make them pop!

To open Google Keep note taking app from the Inbox, be sure the side panel is open by clicking on the arrow at the bottom right.

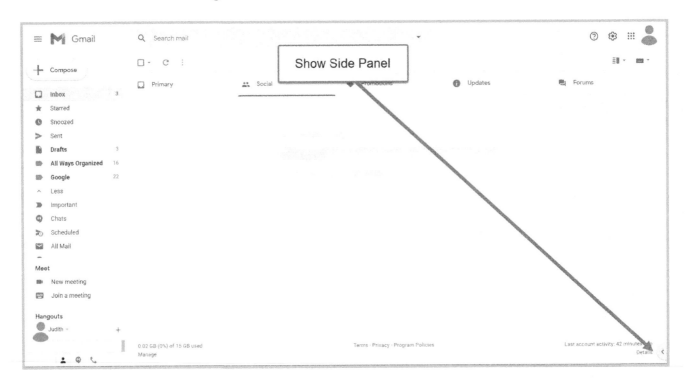

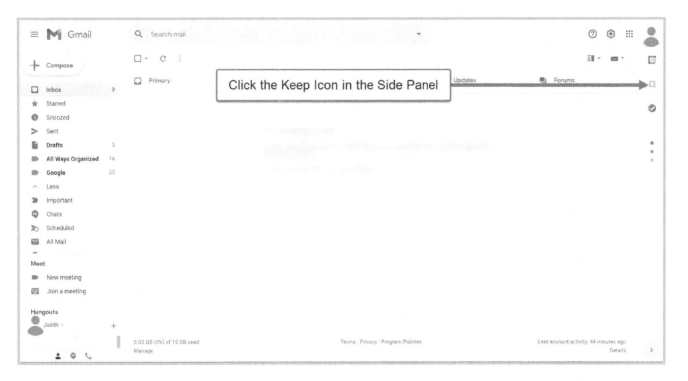

Click on the Google Keep Icon and then on the + to add a new note to Google Keep.

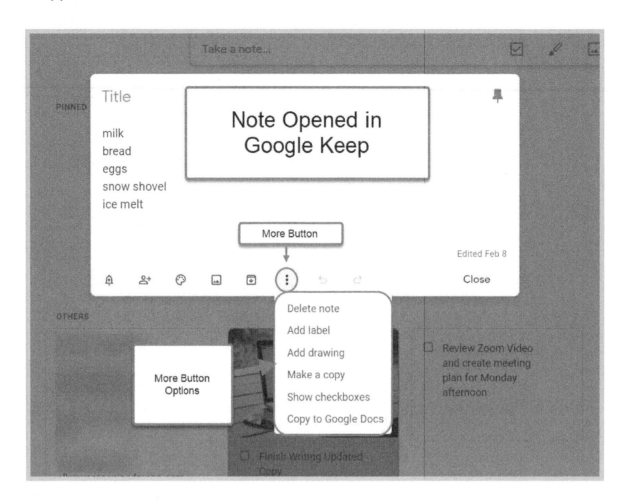

In the Google Keep phone app you can create voice notes. These are great when you are on the go and don't have pen and paper handy. Click on the microphone button on the app on your phone and speak your message. Not only will it save a voice recording, it will transcribe it into text. This text can be sent to a Google Doc—right from Google Keep!

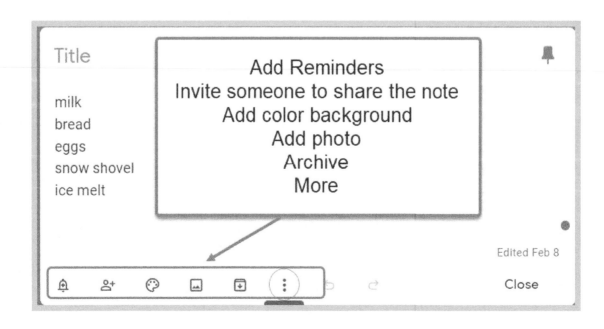

Appendix 5

Google Tasks integration

One of the most powerful tools in a productivity toolbox is a Task list. Now Gmail users have The Google Tasks App available right in the Inbox Window.

First open the Side Panel.

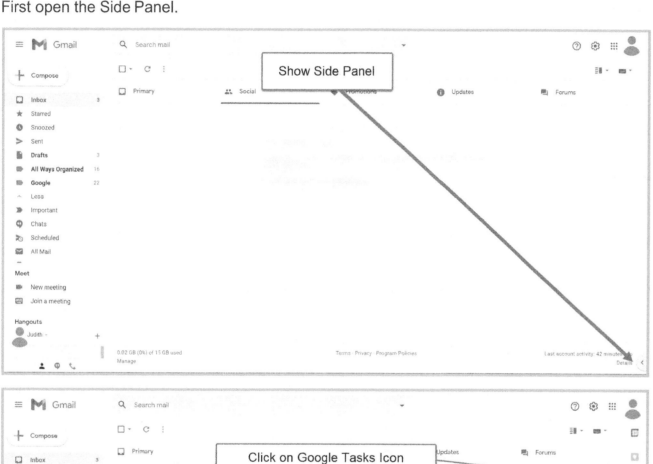

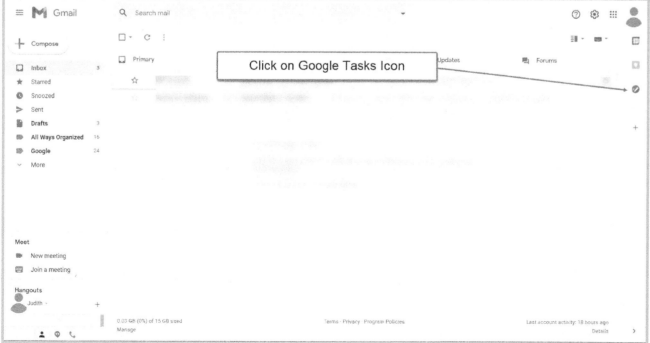

Click the + sign to add a task.

Enter the details.

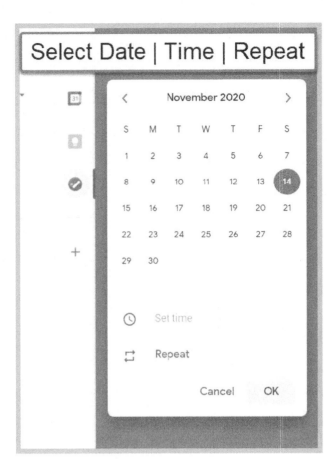

Once all the details are added, click OK.

If you are adding an email to your tasks, click the button above the email text with the check mark. The My Tasks area will appear with the email linked, ready for you to add the details of the task related to this email, including the ability to add date and time, repeat, and any sub-tasks. If you have already created lists of tasks such as personal, business, shopping, party, or any topics meaningful to you, click the list you wish to add the task to and you are all set. By default, you begin with a list called My Tasks. If you do not add your own lists, your task will be stored here.

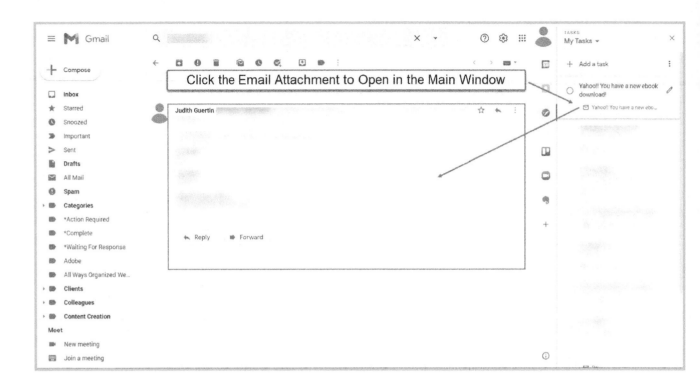

Click the Email Attachment to Open in the Main Window

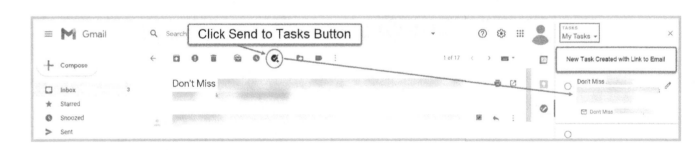

Click Send to Tasks Button

New Task Created with Link to Email

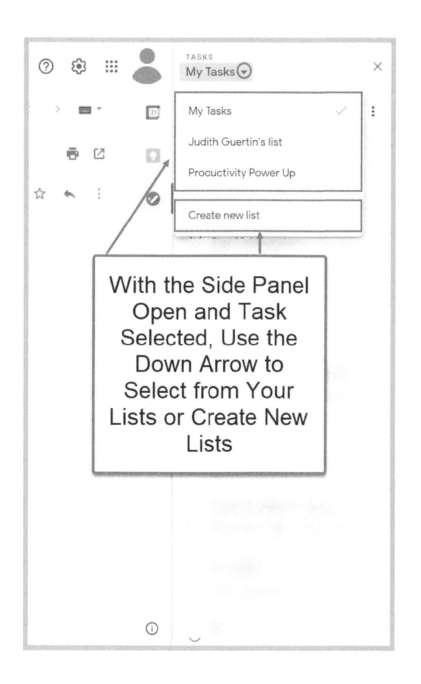

With the Side Panel Open and Task Selected, Use the Down Arrow to Select from Your Lists or Create New Lists

Appendix 6

Google Meet integration

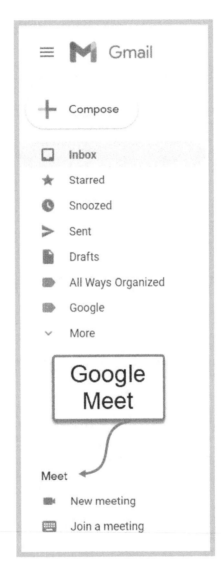

Google Meet is the online video conferencing tool from Google. Recently Google Meet—Start a Meeting, Join a Meeting was added to the lower left-hand side of the Google Inbox. The first time you use this tool, you will complete a brief set up process to give permissions for your camera and microphone as you will see in the following screen captures.

This meeting tool does not require any downloads to your computer. Meet uses the same protections that Google uses to secure your information and safeguard your privacy. Meet video conferences are encrypted in transit and use an array of safety measures to be continuously updated for added protection. Be sure to read and understand all the permissions and policies before using any new tools.

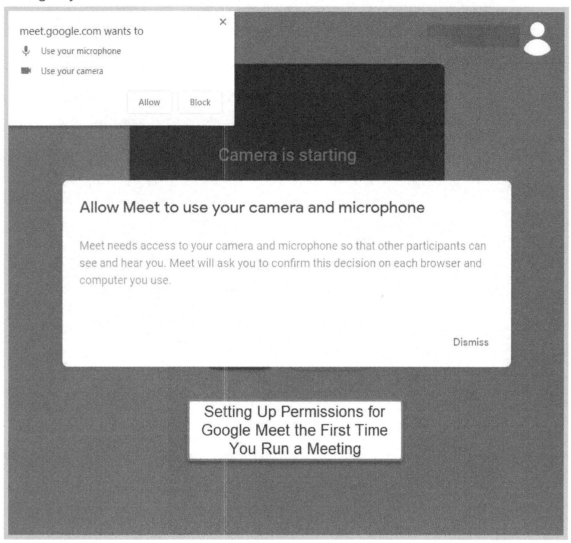

Setting Up Permissions for
Google Meet the First Time
You Run a Meeting

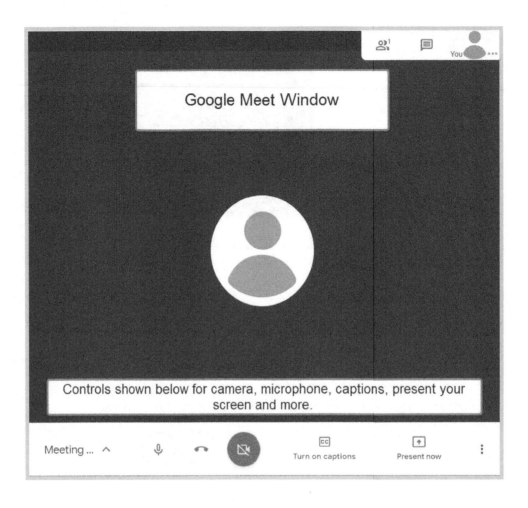

Acknowledgments

First and foremost, my everlasting gratitude to Barbara Hemphill for creating the foundations that are the lifeblood of this work. I am so grateful for her lifelong dedication, not only to creating systems for a Productive Environment™ but also for empowering consultants around the world to do the same, through the Productive Environment Institute.

I have been a follower of Barbara's since starting my business almost twenty years ago. Early in my career, my training came mostly from reading everything I could about organizing. The framework that resonated most was from Barbara's work about Taming the Paper Tiger. I thank her for encouraging me to write this book and for the many hours we spent together, shaping the message of this guide to Gmail.

When I began training in her Certified Productive Environment Specialist program, Barbara shared that her principles would work for organizing anything. This book has given me the chance to showcase her principles in the digital world of Gmail. Her wisdom added substance to every aspect of this guide.

The contributions of friend and fellow Certified Productive Environment Specialist, Ann Thompson, have been nothing short of brilliant. She used her keen eye for structure and context and provided beautiful graphics. She regularly helped to clarify and refine this work. What a great blessing to have her creative input.

I must also mention so many of the other Certified Environment Specialists from the Productive Environment Institute for taking surveys and providing feedback. I especially want to thank Elisabeth Galperin and Kerry Thomas, my esteemed colleagues since early in my Productive Environment Institute journey. I appreciate their wisdom and insights so much.

I also have to mention Catherine Avery, CPES for taking time from her busy schedule to go on a Mastermind Retreat with me to clear the cobwebs and move this work forward at a critical time. It was just the right balance of work, fresh air, and friendship.

Then there is Kathleen Veth, my editor and dear friend. Thank you for all your patience and persistence in the editing process. I have learned so much from your guiding hand and positive spirit.

There are many other authors and productivity colleagues who have inspired me along the way. These include Andrea Anderson, Stephanie Denton, Cheryl Richardson, Judith Kohlberg, Stephanie Nadeau, Denslow Brown, Sheila Delson, Dorothy Lemkuhl, Delores Cotter Lamping, David Giwerc, Angel Crocker, Cal Newport, David Allen, Michael Hyatt, James Clear, and Nir Eyal. During my career in productivity and organizing, the works of each of these individuals arrived at the perfect moment to help shape my journey. I thank you all.

Thank you to Lee Heinrich of Write Way Publishing Company, LLC for helping us realizing the goal of bringing Barbara's Principles to you for the digital age. Your guidance has been so valuable.

Last, I wish to thank my clients. You have all helped shape my vision for how we meet the challenges of working in a growing digital marketplace. Organizing our digital workplace is essential, now more important than ever. I am dedicated to helping you all to understand and flourish in your digital office.

Glossary

7 Information Management Questions: Barbara Hemphill's signature questions for managing documents of any kind—1. Which emails do you need to keep? 2. In what form? 3. For how long? 4. Who is responsible for filing—Archiving? 5. Who needs access to the email you have saved? 6. How can we find it? 7. How is it backed up?

Advanced: One tab of the Settings Area. Selections include: Auto-advance, templates, custom keyboard shortcuts, right side chat, and unread message icon. To turn any of these settings on or off go to the Gear Icon, Settings, Advanced tab.

All Mail: Label for all the email you have stored in Gmail: Sent, Received, Labeled, and Archived.

Archive: Mail you are saving for reference later, stored in the "All Mail" Label.

Asana: A software program used for Project Management. It includes a web and mobile app designed to help teams organize, track, and manage their work. A link to send email from Gmail to this app can be added to the Side Panel of the Gmail Inbox by clicking the plus sign at the bottom of the list of icons on the far right side of the Inbox screen. Use your login credentials and grant permissions requested by Gmail.

Attachments: A computer file added to an email. Documents, photos, PDF files, spreadsheets are some common attachment types.

Auto Correct: A function in Gmail that automatically makes or suggests corrections for mistakes in spelling or grammar made while typing.

Auto Advance: Gmail setting which allows you to move to the next message, the previous message, or back to the Conversation thread after archiving, deleting, or muting an email.

Autocomplete: Typing the first few letters of the name of a saved contact will show matching contacts. Select the address to add in the To: field of an email.

Auto Responder: Vacation Responder is an example of an email response you create and save in settings to be used to reply to email delivered to your Inbox during the time you are away on vacation. Go to Gear Icon, Settings, General Tab, and scroll down to Vacation Responder to complete the message body and details for when to apply this response.

Avatar: The Icon or photo used to represent you on your Google Account. It is on the upper right of your Gmail Inbox.

Blocked Addresses: Email senders you no longer wish to communicate with can be blocked from having their mail delivered to your Inbox. To enable this feature, go to Settings, Filters and Blocked Addresses to add or remove addresses from your list. You can also go to the More button on an individual email (the three dots at the upper right) and select Block to add this sender to the Blocked Addresses.

Box: A cloud-based file storage application that can be added to the Side Panel in Gmail for saving emails and attachments outside of Gmail.

Camera Icon: A graphic of a camera, shown when you click on your Avatar. Use this to change your Avatar Icon to a picture or to update the photo used for your Avatar.

Canned Responses: A template with email body text you use frequently. Create an email response, then click the More button at the lower right of your email, and select Templates to save as a Template. Name it so you can identify it in the list of save templates. To use a template, go to the More button at the bottom right of a blank email (the three dots), select the Template name from the list, edit as needed, and when you finish editing, click send.

Categories: Names of the tabs in your Inbox Type, for example: Primary, Social, Updates, Forums, and Promotions are the categories in the Default Inbox.

Checkbox: The small square next to an individual email, or the small square above the list of emails that select the messages you will work with. Select one email to reply to, or a group of emails to Label, Star, Mark Important, Archive, or Delete.

Cloud: Term used to describe data stored on remote servers accessed from the internet or "cloud." It is maintained, operated, and managed by a cloud storage service provider.

Collaborator: Someone with whom you share documents in Google Docs, Google Sheets, Google Forms among other Google Applications. The Collaborator can edit, comment, or review your document. The edits are tracked and shown in real time.

Comfortable: Refers to a setting for the density of information in your Gmail account. This is one of three choices: Default, Comfortable, and Compact. It refers to how much white space is shown between the emails in the Inbox.

Command: A PC Keyboard key used in concert with other keys to perform functions on the screen without using the mouse. Cmd + B = Bold and Cmd + C = Copy are examples. It is also used to reference Search Operators. When you type search commands into the search box, you find the emails that match the query. Examples are: is:starred, is:important, has:attachments.

Compact : Refers to a setting for the density of information in your Gmail account. This is one of three choices: Default, Comfortable and Compact. It refers to how much white space is shown between the emails in the Inbox.

Composing: Writing an email.

Compose: The button with a large + sign at the top of the Navigation Pane, used to open a new blank email.

Conversation View: All email messages with the same Subject Line, grouped together with the most recent message in the thread at the bottom.

Cost Factors: Space, Time, Energy, and Money

CRM: Customer Relationship Manager.

Customer Relationship Manager: Software program used to record and manage customer relationships.

Customizations: Changes made in the settings area, to personalize the look and feel of the Gmail interface.

Decision Fatigue: A syndrome coined by social psychologist Dr. Roy F. Baumeister. Decision fatigue is the deterioration of our ability to make good decisions after a long session of decision making. The more decisions you make, the worse you will be at weighing all the options and making an educated, research-backed choice.

Decluttering: Removing no longer needed or wanted items from your environment.

Default: The "out of the box settings," of the Gmail interface. The settings in place before you make any changes to customize for your personal preferences.

Desktop Notification: A pop-up window that appears on your computer desktop to call your attention to new incoming email in your Gmail inbox, even if you are not viewing Gmail at the time the messages arrive.

Display Density: Select how closely the emails in your Inbox are arranged. There are three choices in Gmail: Default, Comfortable, and Compact. The setting you choose will determine how much white space you see between emails on the page. Choose the density that suits you best. Change by clicking the **Gear Icon**, then Display Density.

Draft: An unsent email. Gmail stores Drafts in the Drafts Label in the Navigation Pane. Dropbox: A cloud-based file storage application that can be added to the Side Panel in Gmail. Drop-down: A list of options you can select from by clicking on a down facing arrow in Gmail settings.

Dynamic email: A setting that if enabled will allow you to complete tasks without leaving a message: RSVP to an event, fill out questionnaires, browse catalogs, respond to comments, update emails to display the latest content. A lightning bolt icon will identify dynamic email messages.

Email Client: An application on a personal computer or workstation which enables you to send, receive, and organize e-mail. When you send email, it goes from your email client to a central server that routes the email to other email clients.

Events: An appointment sent to Google calendar from Gmail by clicking the More button (the three dots) above an open email message and selecting Create event from the list. Add the date, time, add reminders, invite others to the event, and save to your Google Calendar.

Evernote: A very popular note-taking application developed by the Evernote Corporation. It is available on the Web, PC, Mac, Android. It is used for taking notes, saving web clippings, photos, receipts, documents, PDF's, and more.

Everything Else: An Inbox category name in Gmail. You will find Everything else Category in: Important first, Unread first, Starred first, and Priority Inbox types. This category will include every email that does not match the other categories of the Inbox Type you have selected.

Experimental Access: A Gmail feature that when enabled will give you early access to features under development by Google. A beaker icon will denote these features. Because they are experimental, Google may remove these features without notice.

Feedback: Sending your feelings or reactions to features or issues with a product or how it functions to the maker of the product. Also used to request a new function or feature for the product.

File, Act, Toss System: Barbara Hemphill's signature name for the only three things you can do with a piece of paper: FAT—File for reference, Act on it, or Toss it (Trash, Recycle, or Shred.)

Filters: Sorting and or finding email by using a set of search criteria. Filter by size, by sender, if it contains an attachment, by older than a certain date, contains certain words, sent to a list of email addresses, and many other criteria. See Appendix 2.

Five Sentence Email: Term coined by Guy Kawasaki to describe how long your emails should be. Less than five sentences is too short, and over five is too long. He says that the purpose of an email is to save time, not kill time.

Five Step Productive Environment Process™: The process used by Barbara Hemphill and the members of the Productive Environment Institute to help you create a Productive Environment™, an intentional setting where you can accomplish your work and enjoy your life.

Forums: One of the Gmail Inbox Categories in The Default Inbox Type, where email categorized as from a forum will be sent.

Gear: The Icon shaped like a gear at the upper right of your Inbox. When clicked, it will take you to the Settings area in Gmail. You can configure or change the settings for your Inbox by going to this area.

General Tab: The first tab shown in the Setting Area. To view Settings click on the **Gear Icon** at the upper right of your Inbox. The most common Inbox settings are accessible through this tab.

Google Calendar: The Digital calendar associated with your Google Account. To access while in your Gmail Inbox, open the Side Panel (arrow at the lower right of your Inbox Screen), and click on the calendar icon, located just below your Avatar on the upper right of the screen. Add and edit appointments and events from the side panel or click the double-headed arrow to open the calendar full screen in a new window.

Google Drive: Google's Cloud based storage for your computer files. By default, you have 15 GB of storage in your Google Drive shared by your Google Apps: Gmail, Docs. Sheets, Slides, and Keep, among others.

Google Keep: Google Workspace note-taking application. Available from the Side Panel in Gmail. To access while in your Gmail Inbox, open the side panel (arrow at the lower right of your Inbox Screen) and click on the light bulb icon located just below your Avatar

on the upper right of the screen. Add and edit notes from the side panel or click the double-headed arrow to open Keep full screen in a new window.

Google Tasks: Google's App for creating To-Do Items. Tasks are available from the Side Panel in Gmail. To access while in your Gmail Inbox, open the Side Panel. Add a time to your tasks, view them in Google Calendar, and create repeating tasks.

Google Workspace: The applications created by Google. The most common Google Workspace tools from Google include: Gmail, Drive, Docs, Sheets, Slides, Forms, Calendar, Sites, Meet, and Keep.

Guy Kawasaki: Guy Takeo Kawasaki is an American marketing specialist, author, and Silicon Valley venture capitalist. He describes himself as the former Chief Evangelist at Apple Computers and is now the Chief Evangelist at Canva, the online graphic design service. He coined the term Five Sentence Email and the quote, "The purpose of email is to save time, not kill time."

Help: Support for Gmail is available by clicking the question mark at the upper right of the Inbox Screen.

Horizontal Split: One of the Reading Pane views available to process email in your Gmail Inbox. The other view is the Vertical Split View. Email shown in these views will be marked as read based on your selection in the Preview Pane Setting in the Settings General Tab. Go to the General Tab of the Settings area and select a time frame: Immediately, After 1 Second, After 3 Seconds, After 20 Seconds, or Never.

Hover: Moving your mouse pointer over an area of the screen without clicking the buttons will reveal menus or drop-down choices for you to select.

Icon View: The view of the Navigation Pane, showing only the Icons that represent the Categories and Labels. In this view there is more room for the email itself. This is especially useful when viewing Gmail on a small screen. Click on the three stacked lines next to the Gmail Envelope Icon at the upper left of the Gmail Inbox Screen. When Icons are enabled, hovering the mouse over them will temporarily expand the Icons to include the Category Names in text.

Icons: An icon is a small graphical representation of a program or file.

Images: An image is a picture created or copied then stored in electronic form. There are five types of image files: TIFF, JPEG, GIF, PNG, and Raw Image Files.

Important First: One of the Inbox Types available to use in Gmail. They divide this Inbox type into: Important, and Everything else. Select this Inbox type in the Settings area, General Tab and select this type from the drop-down. A way to select this type without having to leave the Inbox is to hover your mouse over the word Inbox in the Navigation Pane on the left side of the screen, which will reveal a down arrow. Click on the arrow and choose Important first Inbox from the list.

Important Marker: The yellow right-facing arrow you see next to the sender's name in the list of emails in the Inbox. Gmail uses an algorithm to predict if an email is important. They base it on how you have treated similar emails in the past. If you are unsure, why email is marked important, hover your mouse over the email in the list in the Inbox, and it will display the reason. To remove the Important Marker, click on the Important Marker in the list. You can turn this feature off in Settings, General Tab, Important Markers, and select Show Markers or No Markers. Be aware that turning this off will affect the ability to determine the Important email.

Junk Mail: Unwanted or unsolicited email, typically in the form of advertising or promotional materials.

Keyboard Shortcuts: Use the Keyboard instead of using the mouse to perform common functions in Gmail. To turn on this feature go to the Gear Icon, Settings, General Tab, and select keyboard shortcuts on. To learn the shortcuts, go to the "?" at the top of the Inbox Screen and type in Keyboard shortcuts.

Label: A Gmail label is like a tag added to email you receive or send. These labels can keep your inbox organized by allowing you to search based on the Label. They are similar to Folders, however, unlike Folders, you can apply more than one label to a single message. Also, if you delete a label, it does not delete the email that is assigned the Label, only the ability to search using the Label.

Mac: Apple computer with the Mac OS (Operating System) installed.

Maintenance: The processes and procedures used to keep your systems functioning optimally. A regularly scheduled time to review and adjust your projects based on the Five Step Productive Environment Process™.

Methodology: The system used to process your email Inbox. When you process your email, you look at each one, take the next action, and move it out of your Inbox.

More: The three vertical dots that appear at the end of a line of Icons within the Gmail Inbox offering additional actions for a message: Adding events, tasks, filtering messages, mark as unread, and mute are a few of the choices.

Multiple Inboxes: One of the Inbox Types available in Gmail. These are mini inboxes

Google offers within your Primary Inbox. Organize your inbox into sections based on the email type, topic, or personal preference. It's worth noting you can't implement Multiple Inboxes if you're using Gmail Promotions, Social, Updates, or Forums tabs. Select this Inbox type in the Settings area, General Tab and select this type from the drop-down. A way to select this type without having to leave the Inbox is to hover your mouse over the word Inbox in the Navigation Pane on the left side of the screen, which will reveal a down arrow. Click on the arrow and choose Multiple Inboxes.

Naming Conventions: A set of rules, determined by you or your company about how to title email and attachments to aid in searchability. Team members, customers, and vendors should be able to tell at a glance the subject matter of the email, the topic matter, the action requested, or FYI only.

Navigation Pane: The column of Labels at the far left side of the Inbox screen.

Notifications: Options to see pop-up alerts from Gmail when it is open in Safari, Firefox, or Google Chrome Browsers. An alert will pop up when a new email arrives to your Gmail Inbox. Allow notifications for all email, only email identified as Important email, or turn off and receive no notifications. Turn on or off from the Settings area, General tab Desktop Notifications.

Nudges: Using Artificial Intelligence, Gmail scans your email and will return some messages to the top of the Inbox. Nudge identifies important emails in your inbox and tells you the number of days ago it was received and asks if you want to reply, helping you stay productive. See Important Marker.

Obstacles: Anything that impedes you accomplishing your work or enjoying your life. Most often described in terms of space, time, energy, and money.

Offline: The ability to work with messages in the Inbox when not connected to the internet. Messages will be sent the next time Gmail establishes an internet connection.

Paper Tiger Lady: Barbara Hemphill is the founder of The Productive Environment Institute and known as "The Paper Tiger Lady," after her successful Taming the Paper Tiger book series by Kiplinger's.

PC: Abbreviation used for Personal Computer. Most often it refers to computers that run the Windows Operating System.

PDF: Abbreviation for Portable Document Format (PDF Document). It is a universal file format developed by Adobe® that preserves all the fonts, formatting, graphics, and color of any source document, regardless of the application and platform used to create it.

Personalization: Using the Settings of Gmail to customize the look and feel of your Gmail Inbox. Photo: A digital image saved to the computer, added as an attachment or as part of the body text of an email.

Plan: Step four of the Productive Environment Process is to Design and Implement Your Plan. Create the roadmap for achieving your organizing and productivity goals.

Postponed Decisions: Barbara Hemphill based her 40+ year business on four words: "Clutter is Postponed Decisions®." To eliminate clutter, be it physical, digital, emotional, or spiritual, you have to first make a decision.

Preview Pane: Recently renamed the Reading Pane. It is a live preview of the email selected in the Inbox. Act right from this pane. It is shown either to the right of the inbox or below the inbox, depending on your settings.

Primary: One of the Inbox tabs of the Default Inbox Type. It is where your most important emails are displayed.

Print Button: An Icon of a computer printer that will open up a print dialog box. In the dialog box you select what to do with the document: print to paper, to a PDF, save to Google Drive, or many other programs you have installed on your computer.

Priority: One of the Inbox Types available to use in Gmail. They divide this Inbox type into: Important and unread, Starred, and Everything else. Select this Inbox type in the Settings area, General Tab and select this type from the drop-down. A way to select this type without having to leave the Inbox is to hover your mouse over the word Inbox in the Navigation Pane on the left side of the screen. That will reveal a down arrow. Click on the arrow and choose Priority Inbox from the list.

Processing: Applying the File, Act, Toss System™ to your Inbox. There are three choices: file, act, or toss. File what you need later in the Archive with Labels, Stars, and Important Markers. Act on the email by: sending a reply, reply all, forwarding, deleting, creating a task, creating an event, or snoozing it to return to the Inbox later for action. Toss includes: marking email as spam, blocking the sender, sending to trash, and unsubscribing from newsletter lists.

Productive Environment: An intentional setting where you can accomplish your work and enjoy your life™.

Profile Picture: The photo uploaded to your Google account which becomes your Avatar in Gmail and your other Google apps like Docs, Sheets, Slides, Keep, and Forms to name a few.

Project Management: Computer software programs that help project managers (PMs) and teams collaborate and meet goals on time while managing resources and cost. This software is used to track task distribution, budgets, resource planning, team collaboration, and many more.

Promotional: One of the five tabs of the Default Inbox Type. Gmail uses an algorithm to determine the Tab it delivers each email to. In part how you interact with an email can determine whether Gmail will send similar email to the promotions tab. If emails in the tab are not promotions, drag them to the correct tab, or set up a filter to tell Gmail where to send similar messages.

Questionnaires: A set of questions to gain information useful to the sender.

Read Receipts: A response to an email, showing that the recipient has opened the message.

Reading Pane: Previously called the Preview Pane. Enable or disable this view in Settings, Inbox Tab, Reading Pane. View the email message next to the list of inbox emails (either to right—vertical view or below—horizontal view.) Act on the email directly from the reading pane.

Reply: Sending a response to the sender of an email.

Reply All: Sending a response to all the addressees of an email.

Resources: Committing Your Resources is the third step of the Productive Environment Process™. Resources include: space, time, energy, and money.

Rules: A set of criteria you select to create a rule to filter your email. Filters act on the mail arriving to your Inbox. You may set up a rule to add a Label to an email from a particular sender. Another rule could be set to put Newsletters from a certain company in a read later Label, skipping the Inbox altogether. These are only some of the many ways to create and use filters.

Save Changes: The button "Save changes" is at the bottom of each tab in the Settings area for applying the changes you have made to the various settings on each page.

Schedule Send: Gmail feature for selecting a future time to send the message you have written. Click on the down arrow to the right of the blue Send button to reveal the "Schedule Send" option. Fill out the pop-out box with the details and your message will be sent at the time you selected. It will display confirmation at the bottom right of the screen. You will find scheduled messages in the Scheduled Label in the Navigation Pane until Gmail sends them.

Search: Use the Search mail box at the top of your Inbox to find an email by sender, size, date, has attachment, contains certain words or uses a label.

Send: The blue button at the bottom of an email used to send your response when your reply is complete.

Settings: The area accessed by clicking on the **Gear Icon** that allows you to set up your personal preferences for working in Gmail.

Side Panel: Clicking on the arrow at the bottom right of the Inbox reveals icons for Google Calendar, Google Keep, and Tasks along the right side of the Inbox screen. Clicking on these icons opens these Google Apps from the Inbox Screen. Create a calendar entry, a task, or take a note without leaving an email. Add some of your non-Google apps to this Side Panel by clicking the + sign below the Tasks Icon and selecting from the list of apps.

Signature: A block of text added to the end of an email with your contact information. Go to the **Gear Icon**, Settings, General Tab, Email Signature. Change the setting to Signature from No Signature and complete the Signature details in the box. When enabled, each email will automatically include the signature details you provided in the box.

Smart Compose: Predictive writing suggestions appear as you compose an email.

Smart Reply: Suggestions for reply text will appear as you type a reply to a message. Use the tab key to accept the suggested text and continue typing your response.

Snooze: A feature of the Gmail Inbox that will temporarily remove an email from your Inbox and deliver again at a future time of your choice. Select this feature to be sure you will see and act on the email when it is important to do so. If you need it before the Snooze date, you can find this email in the Snoozed Label in the Navigation Pane.

Social: One tab of the Default Inbox Type. Email in this view is from Social Network sites like Facebook, LinkedIn, Twitter, Pinterest, Instagram, among others.

Spam: Unwanted and unsolicited email. If found in your Inbox, open the email, right click on the More button (the three dots) and mark as spam or select block sender to stop the sender's email from reaching your inbox.

Star: An option for adding context to an email. Sort email by the stars assigned to them. Stars have different colors and shapes. There are exclamation points, arrows, check marks and question marks. You can add up to twelve different Stars to your Inbox. Choose from the default choices of: 1, 4, All Stars, or custom select only those you prefer. Find the setup for this feature in the General Tab of the Settings area. Click on one of the default choices or drag the desired stars from the Not in use line to the In-Use line.

Starred First: An Inbox Type in Gmail that orders all email marked with a star to the top of the Inbox View. Gmail places other email in Everything else.

Subject Lines: The first line of text below the sender line of an email that tells the recipient what the email is about. A particularly important aspect of email and often determines whether the email is read and acted upon or sent immediately to the Trash Label.

Systems: The policies and procedures we used to complete projects or tasks. How parts of our business or home work together in a logical, sequential, or orderly way.

Tabs: Gmail divides the Default Inbox into five categories, displayed in five tabs, across the top of the Inbox screen. The Tabs are Primary, Social, Promotions, Updates, and Forums. There are also tabs in the Settings area. These tabs are: General, Labels, Inbox, Accounts and Import Filters and Blocked Addresses, Forwarding and POP/IMAP, Add-ons, Chat, Advanced, Offline, and Themes.

Task View: Clicking on the Tasks Icon in the Side Panel of the Gmail Inbox opens the Task View. Add new tasks, edit the tasks already created, mark tasks as complete, or delete a task from this pane.

Templates: An email template is a pre-defined email layout, that may already include content like images or text. Rather than create a new email from scratch each time, you can use a template as a base. When you select a template to use as the basis of an email design, you are free to make changes and edit. The changes will only take place in that email; they do not affect the original template.

Themes: The look of the background in your Gmail account. By default, the background is white. Gmail offers several templates to choose from by clicking on the Gear Icon and selecting Themes or use one of your own photos as a background.

Trello: A Productivity App Add-on for the Gmail Inbox Side Panel. Click on the + sign and select from the available Add-ons.

Undo Send: A Gmail option to stop an email from being sent for a few seconds after you click the Send button. Configure this in the General Tab of the Settings area. Choose from 5, 10, 20, or 30 seconds. Clicking Send will reveal a box in the lower left of the screen to Undo which will remain visible for the number of seconds selected in the settings area. Examples for using Undo Send: you forgot an attachment, addressed to the wrong person, or regret sending the message.

Unread First: One of the Inbox Types— Unread First. Unopened email will appear at the top of the Inbox Screen under the Category Unread. All other email will be under Everything else.

Unsubscribe: To remove yourself from a mailing list by using the Unsubscribe link at the bottom of a subscription email.

Updates: Patches made to an existing software program to add or change features, address security concerns or compatibility issues with other programs.

Vacation Responder: An email reply that you set up prior to being away from the office to notify people who contact you by email that you are unavailable. You can indicate a person to contact in case of an urgent need and you can report when you will return. Set this up in the General Tab of the Settings area and turn on and off as needed. You have the option to check a box at the bottom of this set up area to select if you only want the response to go to people you have in your Google contacts. This way only people you know will see you are away or unavailable.

Vertical Split: One of the Reading Pane views available to process email in your Gmail Inbox. It shows email to the right of the list of email messages. See Horizontal Split.

Vision: The first step of the Productive Environment Process™ is to establish your Vision. If you are successful in your organizing and productivity project, what will it look like and how will it feel? What will be different in your environment, your systems, your processes?

Web mail: Web mail is an email system that can be accessed via any web browser when connected to the internet. All emails, calendar services, and contacts are hosted on the email service provider's online servers. Some of the most popular free options are Google's Gmail, Microsoft's Outlook.com, and Yahoo Mail.

Zoom: Online meeting platform that can be added to the Side Panel of the Gmail Inbox Screen.

Index

JUDITH GUERTIN

Judith Guertin worked for over two decades as a Registered Occupational Therapist in mental health, physical rehab, and home care, where she helped clients return to full and productive lives. She trained her clients in what OT calls, "skills for the job of living." Judith transitioned to the world of productivity and professional organizing in 2001. After years of watching people struggle with clutter and disorganization in their homes and home offices in her OT work, she knew she could help, but her healthcare role would only allow her to do just so much. Inspired to help people overcome these challenges, she formed All Ways Organized, LLC.

Using her unique perspective as an Occupational Therapist, Judith helps people develop the skills and systems that will sustain them long after they complete their work together. She helps clients stop trying and start doing!

As a Professional Organizer and Productivity Consultant, Judith Guertin, CPES focuses on entrepreneurs, business owners, and sales executives. Together with her clients she creates workspaces that support efficient workflow, effective time management, maximum productivity, and growing profitability.

Judith works side by side with her clients to help them overcome their technology challenges, paper dilemmas, and filing frustrations. She helps them to understand and follow their unique vision to ever increasing success and revenue. No more wasted time looking for lost or missing files. No more lost opportunities from not capturing contacts into a trusted system. Her clients understand how to manage the time they have to get the results they want, in business, at home, and in life.

She is a Golden Circle Member of the National Association of Productivity and Organizing Professionals (NAPO) and the New England Chapter of the National Association of Productivity and Organizing Professionals.

Judith became a member of the Productive Environment Institute in 2013 and was the first consultant to earn Master's Level Certification in the Certified Productive Environment Specialist Training Program™ in 2015.

When the opportunity to work with her mentor and friend Barbara Hemphill, CEO and Founder of the Productive Environment Institute, aka "The Paper Tiger Lady" presented itself, she could not resist working with her to bring Barbara's timeless principles into the digital world!

BARBARA HEMPHILL

Barbara Hemphill started her career in the organizing industry in 1978 with a $7 ad in a New York City newspaper. In 1988 she released her first book Taming the Paper Tiger which became a bestseller and launched her title of "The Paper Tiger Lady."

Barbara is the founder of Productive Environment Institute, with offices in Raleigh and Carolina Beach, NC, and a team of Certified Productive Environment Specialists who work virtually worldwide. Their passion is helping people accomplish their work and enjoy their lives and helping organizations to increase profit, productivity, and peace of mind.

Barbara has been featured on national media platforms including Good Morning America, The Today Show, and CNN Nightly News. She has also been showcased in publications including USA Today, New York Times, Fast Company, Reader's Digest, Real Simple, and Guideposts. She is a contributing writer for Formidable Woman magazine.

Barbara's most recent book, Less Clutter More Life, reveals that physical and digital clutter is a symptom of emotional and spiritual clutter. She is passionate about empowering others to publish books and honored to collaborate with Certified Productive Environment Specialist Judith Guertin to write Taming the Digital Tiger: Gmail Edition.

Made in the USA
Coppell, TX
20 August 2022

81752988R10096